SPORTS IN SCHOOL

The Future of an Institution

SPORTS IN SCHOOL

The Future of an Institution

JOHN R. GERDY
EDITOR

Teachers College, Columbia University
New York and London

Published by Teachers College Press, 1234 Amsterdam Avenue, New York, NY 10027

Library of Congress Cataloging-in-Publication Data

Sports in school : the future of an institution / John R. Gerdy, editor.
   p. cm.
  Includes bibliographical references and index.
  ISBN 0-8077-3971-5 (cloth : alk. paper)—ISBN 0-8077-3970-7 (pbk. : alk. paper)
    1. School sports—United States.   2. College sports—United States.   I. Gerdy, John R.
  GV346 .S66 2000
  796'.071'073—dc21   00-032559

ISBN 0-8077-3970-7 (paper)
ISBN 0-8077-3971-5 (cloth)

Printed on acid-free paper

Manufactured in the United States of America

07 06 05 04 03 02 01 00   8 7 6 5 4 3 2 1

Contents

PART III
Race and Gender in Sport

PART IV
Athletics and Education: A Good Investment?

Acknowledgments

This project would have never happened had it not been for the contributors. Their patience and hard work will always be greatly appreciated. For those whom I considered friends before the project, I appreciated the opportunity to build on that friendship. For those who were not, I am honored to consider them friends now. After my incessant badgering to "get your stuff in," I would understand, however, if any of them thought otherwise.

I also would like to thank Jim Murray for steering me to Teachers College Press. I am deeply indebted to Faye Zucker for believing in the book from the start and for convincing Teachers College Press to give me the opportunity to publish it, and to my editor, John DeSimon, for his thoughtful suggestions, steady guidance, and good humor. I am also grateful that Amy Detjen was there to pick up the pieces and Tareth Mitch who made sure my i's were dotted and t's were crossed.

Many thanks to Dan Spiegel. Without Dan's technical assistance, I undoubtedly would be facing criminal charges for assaulting a computer. His timely offensive rebounds and "kick-outs" for open jumpers also are appreciated.

To our children, Wallace and James, who always keep it interesting.

And to my wife Follin, whose hard work and sacrifice allow me to do what I love to do, I am eternally grateful for your patience and support.

Preface

Participation in sport "builds character" and teaches valuable lessons in ethics and personal responsibility. Sport promotes fair play and loyalty, encourages racial tolerance, provides educational opportunity, and is an avenue for upward mobility. Coaches and athletic administrators are educators concerned first and foremost with the academic and personal development of the young people in their charge. Sport teaches us that it is not whether one wins or loses, but how one plays the game that matters, because the lessons learned on the playing fields can be applied to life.

For these reasons, America has invested heavily in sport. The amount of time, effort, money, and emotion poured into creating and maintaining sports programs is simply staggering. These justifications are particularly prevalent in the case of youth, high school, and college sports. Because these claims have been largely accepted as absolute truths, our tremendous investment in sport as a tool to promote positive educational outcomes rarely is questioned.

But during my career as a high school, college, and professional athlete, and the many years since as an athletic administrator—2 years as director of youth programs at a Young Men's Christian Association (YMCA), 3 years as a legislative assistant at the National Collegiate Athletic Association (NCAA), and 6 years as Associate Commissioner of the Southeastern Conference—I witnessed things that caused me to question these alleged "truths."

Is a coach or parent screaming at a 6-year-old for missing a fly ball a healthy way in which to introduce a youngster to sport? What lesson in sportsmanship is taught by a coach ranting and raving at a referee over an out-of-bounds call? Just how does an athletic scandal or the low graduation rate of student-athletes positively contribute to the image and educational mission of a university? Does an athletic scholarship represent a genuine educational opportunity or simply a chance to be a pawn in a university's quest to generate revenue and television exposure through its athletic program? Could it be that these "truths" are nothing more than myths promoted by the athletic establishment?

What does sport, particularly sport conducted under the banner of an educational institution or that is justified upon an educational basis, represent today? What has it become? Has organized sport in America become more about the egos of those who coach and administer the programs than about the personal development of those who participate in them? Does it promote positive ideals? Or, does sport, in the age of television, corporate sky boxes, and "sneaker deals," represent something far different? In short, does sport contribute in a positive manner to our nation's educational purposes?

The objective of this book is to challenge the long-held justifications of sport being a valuable and relevant aspect of our nation's educational enterprise. To that end, some of the best and brightest minds in the field have been asked to distinguish between truth and myth about the role of sport as a tool to promote positive educational values, and to consider whether our tremendous investment in sport continues to be a sound one. They have been instructed to pull no punches; to tell it as they see it; to give it an "edge."

The chapters in this volume are also about different and, in some circles, unpopular perspectives—unpopular in that assertions regarding the educational value of sport, claims that have been perpetuated by the "old guard" of coaches, athletic administrators, and journalists, and blindly accepted by the public, will be examined to determine whether they are, in fact, true; and different as in the writers who will explore these issues. Generally, the same group of "sport theorists" are asked to write about the same issues, year after year. This volume offers some fresh perspectives. While accomplished in the field, most of the contributors are not widely published, not for lack of ideas or insight, but for lack of opportunity and encouragement. When ideas challenge the status quo, their proponents are not asked by those in the establishment to speak their mind. It is time to hear fresh perspectives—those of different writers, providing new insight on old and often unchallenged "truths" about sport and education.

By the very nature of being different, many of the ideas expressed will be criticized by the mainstream athletic community. Some views may be considered radical. We make no apologies for that. The purpose of this book is not to promote the status quo. Its purpose is to take an honest look at the relevance of sport as a promoter of positive educational values and outcomes. These writers were chosen not only because their ideas are timely and creative, but because they share a common concern. While they believe in sport's potential to successfully meet its educational purpose, they worry that its potential is being wasted. They worry that sport is becoming so disconnected from educational values and foundations that it is in grave danger of becoming educationally irrelevant. Their purpose is to provide a wake-up call to coaches, athletic directors, academic administrators, and others involved in educationally based sports. Their hope is that such open and honest dialogue will contribute to efforts to strengthen athletics' contribution to the goals and missions of our nation's educational institutions.

These authors also know that it is not enough to simply criticize. If criticism is to be valid and responsible, it should be followed by thoughtful suggestions for improvement. While much has been written about the problems of sport, there continues to be a dearth of creative and progressive solutions to those concerns. To that end, they have been asked not only to critically examine various notions regarding the educational purpose and value of sport, but to offer thoughtful, practical, and achievable solutions and initiatives to address the problems they identify.

As we enter a new millennium, it is important that we carefully assess the nature, value, and purpose of sport in our society. If it is deemed to have an overwhelmingly positive impact, particularly when evaluated using educational criteria, then we should invest more heavily in sport. If, however, these purported benefits are disproved, if sport is not meeting its educational purposes, we must reconsider its role as an educational tool. Our educational investment in sport is too large and the stakes are too high to do otherwise.

Introduction

Given its tremendous popularity and influence, it would be easy to assume that sport has always occupied an important place in our educational system. Prior to the mid-1800s, however, organized athletics played virtually no role in the education of our nation's youth. While youngsters undoubtedly participated in loosely structured physical activities or contests that involved running or tests of agility and strength, athletics that even remotely resembled the organized youth, high school, or college sport of today simply did not exist. "To Americans at the beginning of the nineteenth century, there was no obvious merit in sport—certainly no clear social value to it and no sense that it contributed to the improvement of the individual's character or the society's moral or even physical health" (Mrozek, 1983).

American attitudes regarding the value of sport as an educational and character-building vehicle began to change during the nineteenth century. Most explanations of the widespread institutionalization of youth and scholastic sport cite the belief of community and educational leaders that organized athletics could assist in addressing four societal concerns: education, socialization, military preparedness, and health.

Perhaps the most widely accepted justification for organized sports programs relates to their alleged educational and character-building benefits. While the lessons learned in English classrooms and science laboratories were important, it was reasoned that so too could be the lessons learned in discipline, teamwork, and perseverance on the playing fields. It was this perception regarding the value of participation in athletics, which soon became a widespread and unquestioned belief, that made the sponsorship of athletic programs, particularly at the youth and scholastic levels, seem logical.

The public's changing view of athletics also was linked to the fact that America was a nation of immigrants. Accordingly, there existed little in the way of cultural tradition. Many of America's traditions had to be invented—in this case, that participation in sports built character or, more precisely, that "winning," whether in sports, business, or war, was "the American way." It was through athletics that immigrants and minority groups were able to prove they were equal and therefore worthy of a piece of the American dream, the first step in their quest for upward economic and social mobility. Thus, sport's capacity to help socialize a diverse population in American ways was deemed by political, business, and educational leaders as being valuable.

Sport also was thought to be an effective way to train men to defend our country. It instilled toughness, discipline, and an unquestioning respect for authority in participants, all characteristics valued by the military. The obvious health benefits of athletic participation further eased the formal incorporation of organized sports programs into our nation's educational system, as the notion that a sound body contributed to the development of a sound mind gained widespread acceptance.

There was, however, another significant, but not generally acknowledged, factor that influenced the virtual explosion in the number of community and high school sports programs created in the early 1900s: economics.

The fact that our country's dramatic increase in investment in sport paralleled our rise as a world industrial power was no coincidence. History tells us that our nation's educational system and policies have been, and will continue to be, influenced and molded by business leaders. America's corporate and business leaders have a strong vested interest in ensuring that our schools instill in students—all potential future employees—the skills necessary to be productive workers. As America emerged as an industrial power in the early 1900s, business leaders took a very active interest in influencing educational and social reform. The creation of youth sports programs and the incorporation of athletics into educational curricula were part of those reform efforts.

> The emerging industrial base of the American economy in the early decades of this century required workers trained to accept punctuality, dependability, obedience to authority, good health habits, and above all, the notion of hard work as the means to success. Success of course became synonymous with financial success. . . .
>
> The emphasis on practical training was not the only change in the academic curricula of the twentieth-century high schools. There was also a new emphasis on inculcating common values in students. Those values that schools emphasized included patriotism, undoubtedly owing to the two world wars in the first half of the century, and to the perceived need to infuse a sense of national identity into immigrants and first-generation Americans.

Other values taught by schools were those compatible with the industrial, corporate fabric of the United States; values that would make for good workers. (Miracle & Rees, 1994, pp. 181–182)

The great industrialists needed workers to man their factories: workers who were loyal, competitive, who responded to authority, and could work as part of a team. These were the types of character traits that organized sports allegedly instilled in participants. To that end, for example, J. P. Morgan, J. D. Rockefeller, and Andrew Carnegie helped finance the Public School Athletic League in New York. At their urging, and with their financial support, organizations such as the YMCA and Playground Association of America were formed.

The evolution of athletics in higher education followed a similar path. American higher education had been in existence for more than 200 years before the first intercollegiate athletic contest (a boat race between the teams of Harvard and Yale) took place in 1852 and over 230 years before Rutgers and Princeton squared off in the first intercollegiate football contest. The formal incorporation of athletics into higher education had never been seriously considered to that point because early American higher education was deeply rooted in religious principles. To the leaders of the colonial colleges, education was based on rigorous study of the classics and devotion to God, which left no time for "games."

College presidents' attitudes regarding the value of sport, however, began to change in the late 1890s. With an ever-increasingly sports-hungry populace with more disposable income to spend on entertainment, presidents began to recognize athletics' potential to generate resources and visibility for their universities. This trend intensified during the 1930s, when transportation and communications advancements made long-distance travel and radio broadcasts of games part of an expanding sports marketplace. Intercollegiate athletics was no longer regional in scope. With these changes came the opportunity to gain widespread national prestige and visibility, which, in turn, would result in increased financial support.

Despite such high-minded claims regarding athletics' potential to contribute to the academic and personal welfare of participants, its development and acceptance as an influential component of our educational system were largely a result of economic considerations. Why, then, do we continue to justify its existence primarily upon educational grounds? What does our reluctance to address these inconsistencies imply about our personal, community, and educational priorities? Could it be that if we admit that the educational link between athletics and education is weak we then will be forced to act on this apparent contradiction? If so, what measures can be taken to bring athletics into line with our educational values and purposes? These are the questions we must ask as we critically consider the notion of sport and education in the pages to follow.

REFERENCES

Miracle, A. W., Jr., & Rees, C. R. (1994). *Lessons of the locker room: The myth of school sports.* Amherst, NY: Prometheus Books.

Mrozek, D. J. (1983). *Sport and the American mentality 1880–1910.* Knoxville: University of Tennessee Press.

PART I

The Educational Benefits of Sport: Myth or Reality?

A FUNDAMENTAL PREMISE of education in our country is to ask questions and explore ideas, to promote free thought, and to seek truth. It is ironic, however, that in issues relating to athletics, we have continued to allow commonly accepted beliefs, half-truths, and myths to influence educational policy and drive educational decision-making processes. Many of these myths have been promoted by journalists, who typically have been cheerleaders for sport. There also has been a reluctance to challenge "power" coaches and athletic officials to quantify and defend their square-jawed assertions of athletics' value and importance. While the late University of Alabama football coach "Bear" Bryant was correct in pointing out that 50,000 people don't pay to watch English class, the mere fact that sport is wildly popular does not dismiss the need to critically evaluate its wide-ranging effects on our nation's educational goals and well-being.

There are various reasons why schools, universities, and municipalities invest so heavily in sports programs. Most of those justifications relate to sports' potential to positively influence young people—educationally, personally, and in matters relating to character development. While the positive benefits of participation in Little League baseball or college athletics are largely unquestioned, there are those who believe that sport, as currently conducted in America, does little to promote sound educational ideals and healthy personal development. Many of the alleged benefits of athletic participation, they argue, are more myth than reality.

In Part 1, we will explore these myths and realities as they relate to four areas: youth sports, athletics as a character-building activity, the belief that athletes are positive role models, and the validity of another commonly accepted benefit of sport—that college/university athletic programs are a sound business investment.

We begin our examination of these "sports myths" at the point at which young people are introduced to organized athletics. During the past 15

5

years, there has been an explosion of organized youth sports activities. The benefits of these activities—development of communication, teamwork, and social skills, for example—are well known. What is less-well known, however, are the potential costs of such programs—increased pressure to perform at ever-younger ages, a fanatical desire by adult coaches to win, and a senseless lack of sportsmanship by adults and children alike. Bob Bigelow, a former first-round NBA draft pick, examines both the potential benefits and pitfalls of organized youth programs, with special attention to children's physical and psychological capabilities in sport. His treatment of this issue will help parents, coaches, and administrators balance these dilemmas, by offering a practical framework for conducting a youth sports program that places at its center, the needs and capabilities of children rather than the egos of adults.

It is the promise of a fair and honest contest that forms the foundation of athletic competition. Athletic participation naturally enhances a participant's moral and ethical development through the teaching of good sportsmanship. But is it true? In Chapter 2, Sharon Stoll and Jennifer Beller, both of the University of Idaho's Center for Ethics, take on what is perhaps the athletic establishment's most cherished ideal—that participation "builds character." The authors review the growing body of research on the character-building potential of athletics and discuss their own extensive research on the effect of participation in athletics on the moral development and ethical-reasoning skills of athletes. Their results and insights might be surprising.

Are athletes positive role models, particularly as the question applies to the promotion of education and good "character"? Why is it that highly visible athletes have a greater responsibility to be a positive role model than does a teacher, police officer, or parent? What in their background and training qualifies athletes to be effective role models? Not much, according to Todd Crosset, an assistant professor of sports management at the University of Massachusetts, Amherst. In Chapter 3, Crosset examines cultural factors that have contributed to the rise of the athlete as role-model ideal and takes a hard look at the flawed wisdom of promoting athletes as role models.

This part concludes with an examination of what is, perhaps, the most prevalent myth regarding major college athletics: that such programs generate significant sums of money for the institutions of which they are a part. In Chapter 4, I examine the economic realities of college athletics—realities that must be acknowledged, assessed, and confronted before we continue to pump resources into a business venture that is suspect at best.

1

Is Your Child Too Young for Youth Sports
or Is Your Adult Too Old?

Bob Bigelow

In Westchester County, New York, a coach attacks an umpire for calling his son out on strikes. In Rhode Island, several dozen players, coaches, and "fans" (parents) brawl after a U-14 travel soccer game. In Missouri, a basketball official is assaulted by a 12-year-old player and an assistant coach after calling a technical foul ("Abusive Fans," 1994). Add to these horrors the coaches who scream, sideline parents who angrily exhort, and children who do not have as much fun as they deserve and we have a youth sports system that is wildly out of control or, at a minimum, one with badly misplaced priorities.

The widespread nature of such incidences, virtually all of which are instigated by adults, suggests that the environment surrounding our nation's youth sports programs may be more negative than positive. In far too many cases, participation in youth sports does more to turn children away from athletics than to develop a lifelong interest in, and love for, sports. Because of the actions and attitudes of adults, sports are not much fun for many of the close to 35 million kids, ages 3–19, currently playing them (Ewing & Seefeldt, 1991; Ewing, Seefeldt, & Brown, 1997; Howard, 1992; National Sporting Goods Association, 1995).

And the effects of how youth sports programs are conducted will continue to grow, because the number of children who play will not decrease soon. Each year since 1990, over 4 million babies were born. The last time there were as many annual births pre-1990 was 1962, the end of the "baby boom." It has been estimated that America will have over 30 million teenagers by 2005, most of whom will play youth sports.

Our societal investment in sports as a tool to promote health, personal growth, and positive, lifelong attitudes regarding fitness and competition is tremendous. However, because the egotistical needs of parents and coaches to win have come to overshadow the needs of children, who simply want to participate and have fun, it is arguable whether we have managed that investment wisely. Adults are modeling youth sports programs on the values they see as part of college and professional sports programs. Those adult values then are jammed down the children's throats. Rather than forcing children to adapt to games as seen and practiced by adults, those games should be adapted to the needs of children. If youth sports are not designed and conducted for the benefit of the kids and if kids are not having fun playing them, why have them?

Most adults consider such a statement blasphemous. People believe that sports are great for kids, teaching them valuable skills such as teamwork and discipline, promoting positive values such as humility and sportsmanship, and encouraging good physical fitness habits. Most adults also find it hard to believe that many kids are not having fun playing sports. "I played sports as a kid," they say, "and I had a lot of fun." So did I. But we played far less "organized" sports than children do today. Prior to ninth grade, I spent my athletic "career" playing sandlot baseball, informal touch/tackle football contests, and the occasional and very informal game of two-on-two basketball. In fact, I never played organized basketball until the age of 14, as a high school freshman.

My 10-year-old son, on the other hand, has played youth baseball, basketball, and soccer since age 6—fourteen organized "seasons" already—and has also taken a few swim, golf, and karate lessons. My lack of involvement in "organized" youth athletic competition, however, did not seem to hamper my athletic development. I played basketball at the University of Pennsylvania and was a first-round draft pick who played in the NBA for 4 years.

TEACHING CALCULUS

For many years, my approach to involvement in youth sports was not unlike that of most other adults and parents. Two incidents, however, caused me to rethink that involvement.

In 1988, I conducted a basketball clinic for 100 third- and fourth-grade boys in my hometown of Winchester, Massachusetts. The topic was the "pick and roll"—a two-player maneuver designed to create an easy shot. Five minutes into my lecture, it became obvious that my young audience, whispering and restless, was not listening. I ended the lecture. With the clinic finished, the kids dashed for the basketballs and began to hurl them around the gym. I returned home to consider my failed performance.

It wasn't until I saw a television advertisement later that day that I understood why I had failed to reach those children. The advertisement, by a national life insurance company, trumpeted the fact that their policies were now comprehensible—written in plain English. To demonstrate how the policies of other companies were unclear, the ad staged a professor in front of a group of children. On his chalkboard were several arcane calculus formulas. As the professor hustled through his complex explanations, the children's jaws dropped. I had seen those same faces that morning during my lecture. I finally understood that I was teaching "calculus" to children who were incapable of comprehending the subject. What made me more uneasy was thinking how much "calculus" I had tried to teach during clinics over the previous 20 years.

The second incident occurred in August 1992 at a boys' sports camp in Maine. I refer to that day as my youth sports "epiphany." The pick and roll started me thinking; the camp incident activated the alarm. I could not help but notice the way the counselors were interacting with the children, asking questions such as, "How did you feel when you made that play?" and, "What should we do as a team to play better?" Such questions allowed the campers to become a part of the learning process. The camp director informed me that this interactive model had been developed for the camp in the mid-1980s. Specifically, he trained the staff to seek feedback from the children. He said that the camp belonged to the kids and that he founded it to ensure that he would always "give sports back to the children." The alarm sounded.

FINDING ANSWERS

On the ride home from Maine, I thought about "giving sports back to kids." I realized that never, during my hundreds of basketball lectures, had I considered whether my audience of children had the ability to comprehend what I was trying to teach them. I thought of the billions of hours spent by adults every year in activities known as "youth" sports—most of those hours spent teaching skills far too advanced for even the most mature youngsters to comprehend. I thought of my very informal and unstructured youth sports experiences, contrasting them with today's young athletes competing in hundreds of formal games prior to high school. I wondered what all of those formal games meant. Did they develop better athletes? Was all that coaching and instruction achieving its purpose? And, most important, were our youth sports programs conducted for the kids; had we given sports back to the children?

I began to study the topic of youth sports and its effect on child development. My research lead to three distinct conclusions. First, for youth sports programs to be effective, the age-appropriate needs of the children must be met. Second, prior to age 12, children are incapable of understanding their role in team sports. And, third, there is absolutely no correlation between athletic development in children and their potential for athletic success in high school and beyond.

THE NEEDS GAP

When asked why they play sports, children overwhelmingly indicate that winning is a low priority until (maybe) high school. This does not mean that young athletes do not want to win, but simply that they participate to satisfy other needs. Children play sports for other reasons, the most common being, in order of importance, to have fun, to develop skills, to get exercise, and to socialize. For teenagers, the need to win can place as low as between 6 and 12 and at preteen ages winning is virtually never mentioned (Ewing & Seefeldt, 1991, p. 41).

But when adults are queried about their priorities relating to involvement in youth sports, winning places much higher on the list. This obvious "needs gap" leads to the following question: "Whose needs will prevail, the adults' or the kids'?" Unfortunately, in far too many cases, it is the needs of adults that are of primary consideration.

Children's needs also vary by age. A 6-year-old is not a 10-year-old is not a 14-year-old. And children are not miniature adults. The physical, psychological, social, moral, ethical, and emotional needs of children also vary greatly. Perhaps the most common example of programs being structured around adult, rather than children's, needs is that of the All-Star travel team. All-Star teams are an adult need. I have yet to hear of any 10-year-old approaching his or her father and saying, "You know, Pops, I'm better than all the kids my age in town; it's time to challenge the best 10-year-olds from other communities." Yet, the adults who run youth sports programs feel the need to create such teams.

COGNITIVE OVERLOAD

A few years ago, I stopped by the Boston Celtics practice gym. Boston's coach at the time was Chris Ford, a long-time friend. Chris was irate because he had spent most of that day's practice polishing the players' "pick and roll" skills. Apparently, they did not learn their lessons well. After practice, Chris and I chatted about my humbling experiences teaching the pick and roll to young kids. He chuckled and confessed that we were equally unsuccessful teachers. His "kids" were millionaire athletes who were supposed to know better. Yet, they still had trouble grasping and performing a basic basketball technique.

The pick and roll I tried to teach those young children required the understanding of a complex series of concepts and skills. What I did not know at the time was that they were incapable of absorbing the information visually or verbally, much less practicing it on the basketball court. It takes only a minute of watching a youth-league basketball game to recognize children's inability to comprehend team concepts. A young player catches a pass, after which pandemonium breaks loose. Four teammates yell to throw them the ball; five defenders ambush the child to steal it, and parents on the sideline scream, "Pass, shoot, dribble the ball!" The child will throw the ball away quickly or bend over and dribble the ball nervously as one of the sideline parents yells, "Don't be a ball hog!"

With so much to consider, the child is confused and will likely remain so throughout the game, experiencing "cognitive overload." The many cues entering the brain simultaneously cause the youngster's thinking to become muddled. The child cannot possibly discern the multitude of options available, let alone choose the "best" one. Team sports events at the youth level are full of similar instances.

In *Beyond X's and O's*, Jack Hustlar (1985), founder of the North American Youth Sports Institute, writes profoundly about serial skills: the ability to do several skills sequentially. An example of serial skills in sports would be a second baseman attempting a double play. As the ball is hit to the shortstop, the second baseman moves to second base. The ball is thrown by the shortstop and the second baseman catches the ball, touches second base, pivots, removes the ball from his glove, and throws 60 or 90 feet to first base—all with a base-runner obstructing his view.

Despite what we adults may wish to teach or what we believe is important for athletes to learn at an early age, Hustlar suggests that before age 12, and sometimes even later, children are unable to grasp their role in team sports. Concepts such as tactics, strategies, and positions remain abstruse to children.

Jay Coakley, a sports sociologist, described in his book, entitled *Sport in Society: Issues and Controversies* (1986), that what parents and coaches perceive as a young athlete's inability to conform to team concepts is, in terms of child development, perfectly normal.

> Parents and coaches often forget . . . that most children under the age of 12 do not have the cognitive ability to fully grasp the meaning of strategy in team sports. Anyone who has ever watched two teams of 8 year old soccer

players understands what this means. Many children under the age of 12 play what might be called "beehive soccer"; after the opening kick there are 20 bodies and 40 legs within 10 yards of the ball. And they follow the ball like a swarm of bees following its queen. Everyone's out of position and they stay that way for the majority of the game. Meanwhile, many adults on the sidelines loudly plead with their kids to "stay in position" or "get back to where you belong"! But one of the problems in many team sports is that positions change depending on where the ball or other players are. Therefore, the only way players can really determine where they belong is to mentally visualize the relationships between teammates and opponents over the entire field. This ability to visualize all these relationships and think in terms of an overall social system is not often developed before the age of 12.

This inability of children is frustrating to parents and coaches. Without understanding why children have such a difficult time conforming to team strategy, adults accuse them of not trying hard enough, not thinking or having a bad attitude. This, in turn, is frustrating to the young players who are trying and thinking the best they can. Like their parents and coaches, they do not realize that their inabilities conform to normal developmental processes. (p. 238)

DELUSIONS OF PREPUBESCENT GRANDEUR

In December 1978, a 15-year-old, 5'11" sophomore basketball player was cut from the varsity. By his junior year, Michael Jordan was 6'3" and, as a senior, 6'5". As a 6'6" freshman in college, he made the basket to win the NCAA national championship. At age 21, he skipped his senior year to enter the NBA where he was soon recognized, a mere 6 years beyond high school JVs, as one of the five best basketball players in the world. In 6 years, Jordan's body and basketball skills matured exponentially.

Jordan's case is perhaps the prime example of the fact that there is absolutely no way to predict the future athletic skills of preadolescents. Michael Jordan's preadolescent basketball ability (or lack thereof) hardly prevented him from future superstardom. Many of our finest athletes are late bloomers. Yet, parents and other adults continue to be obsessed with the athletic performance of their 8- and 10-year-old children. Such obsession places far too much pressure on a child, often leading to feelings of anxiety, inadequacy, and depression, and certainly takes the fun out of participation in sports.

This reality is difficult for parents and youth coaches to accept, particularly if elementary or middle school-aged children's athletic talent is "ahead" of that of peers. Because a child is "better," parents believe his or her current talents augur future interscholastic, intercollegiate, and professional greatness. However, a prepubescent child's athletic ability is meaningless as an indicator of future athletic ability.

Again, I have been able to call on my own childhood experience to better understand this reality. In my seventh-grade gym class was the finest 12-year-old athlete I have ever seen. He could play any sport better than any of us. He was stronger, faster, and quicker than all of his classmates. He was a brilliant student and accomplished musician. He also shaved.

We dreamed of this 12-year-old athletic wonder leading us to high school state championships in whichever sports he decided to play. But on his way to future interscholastic glory, a funny, and completely natural, thing happened. His classmates began to catch up and, in some cases, surpass him as an athlete. While he dominated me in eighth-grade basketball, by ninth grade I bested him. My dormant, pubescent coordination had awakened. Although he became a fine two-sport high school athlete, he never played college sports.

Any high school coach can give you numerous examples of early talents fading into the athletic woodwork. Millions of preadolescent "superstar" ninth graders become average seniors. Conversely, freshmen who are barely coordinated become All-Staters as seniors. The random onset of pubescence in kids ages 9–16 ensures that prognosticating future athletic ability is a roll of the dice.

The inability of parents and youth coaches to understand or their refusal to accept this developmental reality is the cause of the most urgent problem in youth sports—the segmentation of youth athletes of the same age by athletic "ability." Whatever they are called—travel teams, all-star teams, select teams, A-B-C-D, 1-2-3, Major–Minor, AAA-AA-A—their purposes are the same: the sifting and/or cutting of young athletes.

The practice of cutting children from teams or creating elite travel teams is an extremely controversial and emotional issue. Parents whose children make the "top" team usually support such practices, while the parents whose child has been cut oppose them, questioning the system's validity or the coach who did not choose their offspring.

As in the case of Michael Jordan, or in my case, prepubescent athletic performance provided no indication of future performance. The current relative ability of any group of children most likely will change when it is re-evaluated 6 months, 1 year, or 3 years later. Why, then, create a system that discourages young children from continuing to participate in sports? And if we truly believe in all of the supposed fitness, character, and educational benefits of athletic participation, wouldn't we want all children to participate, regardless of their athletic skill level?

How many children have been cut, sifted, and demoted before their bodies matured? How many children have become frustrated and perhaps quit a sport, never to try again after being told they were not good enough to make the team at age 8? The uncoordinated kid who is cut at age 12, if encouraged and provided the opportunity to stay involved, may develop into an outstanding athlete. Regrettably, in many cases, we will never know if he or she would have.

"What is the real reason behind select teams under 12 years old?" asks Ric Granyrd (1993), past Coaching Director for the South Texas Youth Soccer Association. "I find it very difficult, nay impossible, to tell a youngster he or she is not good enough for a team. Heck, these youngsters are ten year olds! How good can they be at anything yet?" (p. 42).

Dr. Lyle Micheli, nationally-renowned expert on childhood injuries in sports, describes the problem as follows:

> Two controversial issues in children's sports involve benching and cutting of players. Coaches who regard winning as the most important element in children's sports are known to cut even eight-year-olds from teams. One of the first questions I ask my young patients is how they're enjoying sports. Almost nothing makes me feel so bad as when a child looks at me with a crestfallen face and tells me he was cut because he "wasn't good enough." It's absurd we should encourage children to try out for a team and then exclude them at the outset. Children don't need to learn these brutal lessons of life—"survival of the fittest" and so on—at this early stage. I see absolutely no reason why *any* child should be prevented from taking part in a program, if he or she is healthy enough, particularly before the age of fourteen. (Micheli & Jenkins, 1990, pp. 135–136; emphasis in original)

Why create a system that cuts 8-year-olds? As mentioned earlier, in many of our nation's youth sports programs, the needs of adults prevail over the needs of children, the selection of all-star or elite travel teams being a prime example. In short, we have let organized youth sports get into the hands of adults who don't know better, or don't know a better way.

PRESCRIPTIONS FOR REFORM

What can be done to reform youth sports programs to give them back to the kids? Obviously, parents, youth coaches, and the administrators who run those programs should consider these prescriptions. But so should others. High school coaches and administrators have a tremendous impact on the tone of youth sports programs in their towns. Even college coaches, administrators, and educators can influence the way in which we think about the role of youth sports in our country. The entire sports industry has a stake in ensuring that our youth sports programs are run in a manner that provides for the enjoyment and meaningful participation of all children. In short, youth sports should be fun, and we all have a stake in helping to make it so.

Thus, the following suggestions:

1. *Eliminate all travel/select/elite/all-star groupings and teams through sixth grade.* There is simply no need for all-star travel teams at such an early age. Labeling children as either "good" or "no good" is unhealthy. A local high school team's talent will not suffer one bit and the sports world won't collapse if the area's best group of 10-year-old soccer players remains undetermined. Even Pele, the world's greatest soccer player, has said that selecting the "best" players for special traveling teams before the age of 14 is too early("Youth Programs," 1998). Why discourage a child who might not be considered "good enough" at age 10 from staying involved in sports? Who knows, that "no good" might one day mature into "the best." Thus, all elite travel teams through sixth grade should be eliminated. Let the kids stay at home and play with their buddies—they'll probably have more fun.

2. *Volunteer for Special Olympics.* Each youth sports board member, coach, or parent should be encouraged to spend a day volunteering at the Special Olympics. While assisting these "special" athletes striving in challenging circumstances is reason enough to volunteer, such involvement can teach a great deal about keeping sports in the proper perspective. The Special Olympics' motto is terrific: "Let me try to win, but, if I cannot, let me be brave in my attempt." This motto should be written on signs at every youth sports venue. All children who play should be rewarded for their participation and effort.

3. *Require training for coaches.* As will be discussed in Chapter 5, the majority of youth sports coaches are people whose only credentials are being a parent or having an interest in sports. Often, their only training consists of what they observe of coaches on television or what they remember from their own athletic experience. The problems that arise due to the lack of formal preparation of youth coaches are significant. Thus, youth sports organizations must develop a formal orientation and training program for their coaches, designed to provide them with a solid knowledge base to help them perform their coaching responsibilities effectively. Various models and standards for such programs exist. Youth sports boards must require their coaches to participate in them.

4. *Evaluate coaches based on the following guidelines: (a) They must like kids; (b) they must be able to act like kids; and (c) they must be devoid of self-importance.* It may be comforting if your child's coach knows something

about dribbling or goaltending. However, in coaching children, that technical mastery is secondary compared with these three criteria. Many technically gifted coaches behave boorishly—they like coaching, not kids.

5. *When coaching practice sessions, remember elementary school recess.* The second half of any youth sports practice session should be modeled after elementary school recess periods. During recess, children are neither coached nor instructed. The teachers supervise, ensure children's safety, and settle the occasional fight. Similarly, coaches and parents should let the children choose sides, play miniature games, and modify their contests to suit their pleasures. The adults should stand on the sidelines and supervise but should not coach, teach, or officiate. Parents and coaches simply should organize the time but "unorganize" the process. This technique puts the "play" back in the kids' hands. The result is that the children have an opportunity to build their confidence as well as their decision-making and mediating skills, because adults are not dictating the terms and conditions of play.

6. *During games, switch coaches halfway through the contest.* Changing coaches at half time serves to eliminate coaches' egos from the game, as both coaches win and lose the same game.

7. *Smile.* If any adult (coach, parent, board member) at any youth athletic activity—game, practice, tournament—cannot smile 90% of the time, he or she should be asked to leave. The children don't need or want that person around. There is absolutely no reason why adults cannot smile and enjoy these activities for what they are—games for children. I have seen hundreds of "0% smilers" and they are excruciating to watch. I find myself not smiling 90% of the time I watch them.

YOUTH SPORTS FOR KIDS, NOT ADULTS

Our society believes very strongly in the perceived benefits of children being involved in sports. Not only are sports fun, but they build character, teach values such as hard work and discipline, and promote positive fitness habits.

But do our youth sports programs do these things? Are children having fun playing them? Is our investment in youth sports reaping positive dividends? As will be articulated by various other authors in this book, it is not sport by itself that contributes to the personal and educational development of our nation's youth. Rather, it is the environment within which athletic activities occur that influences such development. If youth sports programs are not designed and conducted with the needs of children foremost in mind, if children are not having fun playing sports, and if adults are too interested in satisfying their egotistical or competitive desires, then we would be better served by eliminating these programs.

The success of organized youth athletics programs depends on their being conducted in an environment designed to meet the personal, athletic, and educational needs of children. Such programs must be conducted to meet the needs of all participants—not just the top two, six, or 20, not just your child, not just your neighbor's kid; but the needs of all children—the skinny, fat, tall, small, and the ones who lack highly developed motor skills. Youth sports programs must serve all participants, not just the "special" few. Meeting the varied needs of 10 children is difficult. And to accomplish this successfully in a program with hundreds of children, the task is Herculean, maybe even impossible. But regardless of the difficulty in meeting such needs, these needs must be the focus of such programs, not, as is all too often the case, those of the adults who run them.

For youth sports to be successful, their focus must be to develop better and healthier kids, not to create superstar athletes or serve as a farm system for the local high school team. The purpose of these programs must be to introduce children to competitive athletics on their own terms, not terms created and dictated by adults. In short, it is time for adults to give youth sports programs back to the kids.

REFERENCES

Abusive fans lead amateur umpires to ask courts, legislators for protection. (1994, August 1). *The Wall Street Journal,* p. B-1.

Coakley, J. (1986). *Sport in society: Issues and controversies.* St. Louis: Times Mirror/ Mosby College.

Ewing, M. E., & Seefeldt, V. (1991). *Participation and attrition patterns in American agency-sponsored and interscholastic sports.* East Lansing: Michigan State University, Institute for the Study of Youth Sports.

Ewing, M. E., Seefeldt, V., & Brown, T. (1997). *The role of organized sport in the education of children and youth.* New York: Carnegie Corporation.

Granyrd, R. (1993, November–December). *Soccer Journal,* p. 42.

Howard, D. R. (1992). Participation rates in selected sport and fitness activities. *Journal of Sport Management 6*(3), 191–205.

Hustlar, J. (1985). *Beyond X's and O's.* Welcome, NC: Wooten Printing.

Micheli, L. J., & Jenkins, M. D. (1990). *Sportswise: An essential guide for young athletes, parents and coaches.* Boston: Houghton Mifflin.

National Sporting Goods Association. (1995). *Sports participation in 1994.* Mt. Prospect, IL: Author.

Youth programs. (1998, January 22). *USA Today,* Section C, p. 6.

2

Do Sports Build Character?

Sharon K. Stoll

Jennifer M. Beller

The notion that organized, competitive athletics could be used by schools to supplement the educational development of youth originated with a group of English school masters in the early 1800s. Participation in physical activity, especially competitive activity that is bounded in rules, it was thought, made the players "better people" (Mangan, 1981). Common sense suggested that if the boys were busy on the fields of play, it kept them out of other deeds that might be detrimental to their "gentlemanly" education and contributed to the development of positive characteristics such as sportsmanship, leadership, and discipline.

From these origins, the belief that sports developed positive character traits grew to where the claim is now almost universally accepted by educators, parents, and participants, despite the fact that there is virtually no empirical evidence to support it. The idea that "sports build character" has gained widespread acceptance, not through proof of research, but rather through the personal testimony of coaches and participants.

DEFINING CHARACTER

"Character" can mean different things to different people. Aristotle said that character is the composite of good moral qualities, whereby one shows firmness of belief, resolution, and practice about such moral values as honesty, justice, and respect. He also said that character is right conduct in relation to other persons and to self. Our humanness, he continued, resides in our ability and capacity to reason, and virtue results when we use our reasoning ability to control and moderate our self. Lickona (1991) built on Aristotle's theme to broaden the definition as follows:

"Good character consists of knowing the good, desiring the good, and doing the good—habits of the mind, habits of the heart, and habits of action" (p. 50). Unlike Aristotle, Lickona argues that reasoning is inadequate by and of itself; one must have a strong value system that resides in the psyche but that also is understood and can be articulated. To say, "Cheating is wrong," is inadequate. One must know why it is wrong and put into action what one values, knows, and reasons is right. It is easy to say that one does not cheat but another thing not to cheat when surrounded by others who are cheating.

Shields and Bredemeier (1995) further developed the definition of character as "the possession of those personal qualities or virtues that facilitate the consistent display of moral action" (p. 192). All of these definitions identify the importance and valuing of certain beliefs such as honesty, trustworthiness, and being just, respectful, and civil. Character, then, in an ethical sense, is the sum of the principles, the valuing of the principles, and the behavioral action of the agent while following the principles (Frankena, 1973).

Many involved in athletics might consider the above definition too narrow, particularly as it applies to the traits that athletics allegedly teaches. They would argue that the definition should be broadened to include the sum qualities of being able to work hard, sacrifice for the cause, and be loyal, ambitious, cooperative, intense, and dedicated. While these traits are admirable, an individual who possesses them can be immoral and even dangerous if he or she does not possess the moral virtues of honesty, justice, respect, and compassion. A thief could be dedicated, intense, and ambitious. Bormann, Himmler, and Goebbels were loyal and cooperative to Hitler's Final Solution (Sereny, 1996). Without the virtues of honesty, justice, respect, and compassion, social values are meaningless and character is without a soul.

Character also is often confused with intellect. If an athlete is intelligent and "field smart," it is said that he or she has great character. Yet, intellect, by itself, is not a condition for character. History is replete with brilliant and charismatic leaders who had little moral intelligence (Sereny, 1996). Intellect, if not bounded by the notion of respect, love, compassion, fairness, and honesty, is a demon ready to spring. As Theodore Roosevelt said, "To educate a person in mind and not in morals is to educate a menace to society" (Lickona, 1991, p. 3).

Over the past 10 years, we have engaged in an intensive study of athletics and character, leading to the development of our own definition of character: Character is the ability to be honest, fair, and civil . . . even when no one is watching and even when no one else is practicing ethics (Stoll & Beller, 1995).

DOES ATHLETICS DEVELOP CHARACTER?

In the 1950s, researchers began to study whether participation in sport did, in fact, "build character." Measuring athletic participation's effect on character was not easy. The challenge of defining it proved difficult, as character often was confused with social traits rather than moral traits (Sage, 1988). Developing instrumentation that could answer the question validly and reliably, or, more specifically, measure moral development or moral reasoning, was also difficult. Despite these challenges, the resulting research has been clear and consistent. In empirical designs, a constant was found: Sport does not appear to develop character—no matter how defined.

Research indicates that an athlete's moral reasoning becomes more "masked" the longer he or she participates in competitive athletics. This "masking" of moral reasoning in athletes is the direct result of how sport is conducted in America. "Do whatever you gotta do to win" seems to be the fundamental principle upon which athletics is practiced today. This notion of "masked" reasoning has been termed "moral callousness."

> Just as callouses on our hands prevent us from feeling what we touch with much sensitivity, moral callouses that form around our hearts keep us from feeling issues of ethical right and wrong. (Kretchmar, 1994, p. 238)

Kretchmar argues that the following are common symptoms of moral callouses:

- frequent appeals to the fact that "everyone is doing it" (therefore, how could it be wrong?)
- an inability to distinguish between what is part of the game and what is not (if there are no penalties in the rule book for behavior x, behavior x must be part of the game)
- difficulty in telling morally sound strategy from win-at-all-costs trickery (some blatant rule breaking is now referred to by TV commentators as shrewd strategy)
- a sense that if one is not caught, nothing wrong happened (whatever works is right)

Apparently, the result of continued participation in highly competitive, win-at-all-costs athletics is a morally calloused, "hardening of the heart" attitude that manifests itself in a lack of cognitively respecting, honoring, and showing dignity toward fellow competitors, teammates, rules, and the spirit of the game. Other than an isolated study or two

(Bredemeier & Shields, 1986), research has found that nonathletes use a significantly more principled and less calloused approach to addressing moral issues both in the sports arena and in societal contexts (Beller, 1990; Beller & Stoll, 1992, 1995; Beller, Stoll, Burwell & Cole, 1996; Hahm, 1989; Krause & Priest, 1993; Penny & Priest, 1990).

Regardless of the research results, influential coaches and sport advocates continue to promote sports' character-building qualities. "The research is flawed," they claim. "They weren't measuring what they thought they were." "Character can't be objectively measured" (Gough, 1993; McGinnis, 1993). For the most part, the public has blindly continued to believe in sport as a valuable character-building activity.

CURRENT RESEARCH

Given the continued misconception regarding the debate over whether sports build character, we began to examine the question more extensively. Our studies were based on the Kohlbergian (1981) notion that moral behavior is rooted in moral reasoning. As Aristotle noted, without the reasoning process, virtue is meaningless. One does not engage in virtuous action if one doesn't understand the importance of virtue. Such an individual is a mimic, not an agent of moral activity.

The two instruments that typically are accepted as the empirical standards for evaluating athletes' and general students' cognitive moral-reasoning ability are the Hahm–Beller Values Choice Inventory (Hahm, Beller, & Stoll, 1989) and the Defining Issues Test (Rest, 1979).

The Hahm–Beller Values Choice Inventory (HBVCI) evaluates, from a deontological or ideal philosophy, how individuals use principles to reason about commonly occurring moral issues in sport. Evaluation of the reasoning process is based on "the ability [of respondents] to systematically think through a moral problem taking into consideration one's own values and beliefs while weighing them against what others and society values and believes" (Lumpkin, Stoll, & Beller, 1994, p. 1). Using a Likert scale of strongly agree to strongly disagree, subjects responded to 21 scenarios relating to issues of retaliation, drug use, personal responsibilities for actions, fairness to teammates and opponents, and the intentional foul. The higher a HBVCI score, the more impartially, reflectively, consistently, and ideally an individual reasons across all inventory questions.

The Defining Issues Test (DIT) evaluates moral-reasoning ability using hypothetical moral issues in a social context (Rest, 1986). The scenarios are founded in Kohlberg's (1981) cognitive moral development theory and deontological ethical theories. To decide a course of action, respondents reason through six hypothetical moral dilemmas and rate the importance of the moral issue statements. The higher the DIT score, the higher the moral "principled level of thinking" used by the respondent. These principles are daily guidelines that we develop based on our personal value and belief structures and are consistent with universal principles such as respect for private property, for the truth, and for others (Beller & Stoll, 1995).

After choosing these instruments, our challenge was to test a large enough number of athletes and nonathletes to ensure that our results would be statistically sound. To that end, we evaluated over 40,000 general students and team and individual sport athletes—from youth, interscholastic, and intercollegiate (Division I–III) sport; cadet teams at the U.S. Armed Forces Academies; Olympic levels; and colleges with a Christian mission and focus.

MORAL-REASONING RESEARCH FINDINGS

Closer scrutiny of the results of our HBVCI research over the past 10 years indicates that male team sport athletes generally have scored significantly lower than individual sport athletes (Beller, 1990; Beller & Stoll, 1995; Beller, Stoll, Burwell, & Cole, 1996; Carrodine, 1993; Hahm, 1989; Krause & Priest, 1993; Nelson, 1993; Penny & Priest, 1990; Stoll & Beller, 1989). Similar findings hold true for female team sport athletes, who score lower than their individual sport athlete counterparts (Beller, 1990; Beller & Stoll, 1992, 1993a, 1993b, 1994, 1995; Beller, Stoll, Burwell, & Cole, 1996; Hahm, 1989; Krause & Priest, 1993; Penny & Priest, 1990). Despite claims and anecdotal accounts of the importance of participation in team sports for the development of "character," evidence mounts that team sport athletes appear to be more morally calloused than either their individual sport or nonathletic peer groups.

Effects of Competition on Moral Reasoning by Gender

Prior to 1988, few researchers had systematically evaluated female athletes' moral reasoning. Studies by Bredemeier and Shields (1984, 1986) and Hall (1981) found that females scored higher than males on moral reasoning. Two additional studies using the DIT (Hahm, 1989, and Beller, 1990) found that female athletes scored higher, although not significantly higher, than male athletes.

Results of more recent research using the HBVCI (with approximately 15,000 female athletes in more than 35 studies) have been fairly consistent. Other than one study (California State University Fullerton Department of HPERD, 1994), female athletes scored significantly higher than male athletes (Beller, 1990; Beller & Stoll, 1992; Beller, Stoll, Burwell, & Cole, 1996; Hahm, 1989; Krause & Priest, 1993; Kretchmar, 1993; Nelson, 1993; Penny & Priest, 1990; Stoll & Beller, 1991, 1992, 1993; Wadilow, 1994). While these results appear to support the argument that females are not as morally calloused as their male peers, a closer longitudinal examination of the data paints a disturbing picture.

An analysis of female athletes over the past 10 years revealed that their moral reasoning is becoming more calloused. Other than one study at Christian colleges (Beller, Stoll, Burwell, & Cole, 1996), where females scored in the low 70s on the HBVCI, the mean scores for female collegiate athletes from 1988 to 1990 were in the high 60s. From 1991 to 1993 female athletes' scores averaged in the mid-60s, while studies from 1994 to 1999 find scores averaging in the low 60s, indicating a steady erosion of their moral reasoning skills.

Results of studies of interscholastic female athletes are similar. A study published in 1995 (with data collected from more than 1,300 students in 1990–91 in one of the largest school districts in the country) revealed that female athletes scored in the high 60s (Beller & Stoll, 1995). In contrast, a 1997 study of interscholastic athletes (in different geographical sites throughout the country) found that the mean scores were in the low 60s (Beller, Stoll, & Rudd, 1997), again indicating an erosion of moral reasoning.

The above trends also applied to athletes and nonathletes at colleges with a stated Christian mission and focus. In a study evaluating 360 athletes and nonathletes at four such schools, nonathletes scored significantly higher than team sport athletes but not significantly higher than individual sport athletes. Moreover, female nonathletes scored significantly higher than both male and female team sport athletes (Beller, Stoll, Burwell, & Cole, 1996).

Results of Competition on Athletes' Moral Reasoning by Educational Attainment

Perhaps the difference between athletes' and nonathletes' moral-reasoning ability is tied to educational attainment. Both the U.S. Military and Air Force Academies have evaluated their incoming cadets using the HBVCI. These freshmen are selected not only because of high school academic excellence (from the upper 3–6% of high school graduates nationwide), but also because they allegedly demonstrated moral values such as honesty, responsibility, and justice. Of interest is that these studies revealed that incoming cadets' moral-reasoning scores reflect the findings in studies of general university athletes (Krause & Priest, 1993; Penny & Priest, 1990; Wadilow, 1994). Cadets who were recruited as intercollegiate athletes were more morally calloused than nonintercollegiate athletes.

Moreover, the previously mentioned colleges with a Christian mission generally have high academic entrance requirements. Thus, it appears from these studies that educational background does not affect how well an individual reasons about moral issues. These findings support Rest's (1986) analyses of studies with the DIT showing that educational attainment does not correlate to moral reasoning.

RECONSIDERING PHILOSOPHY

If one of the primary justifications for athletics is that it builds the "character" of participants, then we must all—practitioners, coaches, parents, and participants—reconsider the role of sport in our educational system. Despite the anecdotal accounts and personal testimony regarding sport's role in character building, research indicates that sport, as currently conducted in America, does not appear to develop character. Forty years of research, conducted by more than 20 researchers studying tens of thousands of athletes and nonathletes from the youth, high school, collegiate, and Olympic levels, simply does not support the notion of sport as a character-building activity, particularly as it applies to sportsmanship behaviors and moral-reasoning ability. Studies examining elementary and junior high athletes and other students have consistently found negative relationships between sportsmanship behaviors and the length of involvement in sport (Boyver, 1963; Dubois, 1986; Hansen, Beller & Stoll, 1998; Lakie, 1964; Olgilvie & Tutko, 1971). Research involving intercollegiate athletes has found that they are significantly less mature in their moral reasoning than their peer group (Allison, 1981; Bredemeier, 1984; Bredemeier & Shields, 1986; Hall, 1981; Kistler, 1957; Kroll, 1975; Kroll & Petersen, 1965; Richardson, 1982).

In short, research continues to support Olgilvie and Tutko's (1971) earlier, although much contested and largely not accepted, work concerning the effects of competition on personality.

> We found no empirical support for the tradition that sport builds character. Indeed, there is evidence that athletic competition limits growth in some areas. . . . Athletic competition has no more beneficial effects than intense endeavor in any other field. (p. 60)

While the evidence is strong regarding the negative effect of participation in sport on character, there is hope. Research in character education has proven that the reasoning processes that Aristotle described can
be learned and developed. Research findings in leadership are also clear
that character can be supported through environments that challenge and
demand ethical practices. Hence, there is no reason why an intense activity like sport could not develop, support, and foster moral character.

A PLAN OF ACTION

Developing moral-reasoning skills is a lifelong process, affected by environment, education, exposure to role models, and the media. As research
builds suggesting that the environment surrounding our nation's athletic
programs actually hinders the development of ethical- and moral-reasoning skills, the question becomes, What can be done to restructure such
programs in a way that promotes the development of positive moral- and
ethical-reasoning skills in participants? Following are suggestions:

1. *Development of Program Philosophy.* The fundamental purpose and philosophy of our sports programs must be not only clear, but, more important, clearly articulated to all participants, including coaches, parents, athletes, media, and the public. Specifically, we must determine
   what athletics is about. For example, youth, high school, and college
   programs are justified, in large part, by their alleged positive contribution to the educational institution of which they are a part and to the
   personal and educational development of participants. But have such
   programs become more about generating revenues and winning at any
   cost? If so, should such programs continue to be sponsored by educational institutions? How can we expect that participation in athletic
   programs will develop positive character traits of sportsmanship, honesty, compassion, and ethics if the fundamental program philosophy
   is driven by win-at-any-cost principles and attitudes? If our athletic
   programs are to be about education and the personal and ethical development of those who participate, then our program philosophies must
   clearly reflect those priorities. The development of a program philosophy statement is the first step in creating an environment where positive educational development and ethical behavior are encouraged
   and valued.
2. *Development of Ethical Standards and Codes of Conduct.* After a program's
   broad philosophical principles have been agreed upon, specific stan-

dards of behavior must be outlined and articulated in a code of conduct. Such a code helps the individual place the broad philosophical
program principles into a specific behavioral context. If, for example,
we want coaches to display behavior that promotes principles of good
sportsmanship, it is imperative that behaviors, actions, and attitudes
that promote those ideals be clearly and specifically outlined.

3. *Development of Educational Programs.* The development of a philosophy
statement and a code of ethics are only the the first steps in building
an athletic program that instills in participants a strong sense of ethical
and moral responsibility. Using these principles as a point of reference,
athletic programs must then develop educational and professional development initiatives to ensure that coaches, parents, athletes, media,
and the public understand and develop their own ethical- and moral-
reasoning skills. If our athletic programs are to be "about education,"
we must provide coaches and administrators opportunities to further
develop and refine their skills as educators. It is not enough to trust
that coaches, athletes, parents, or fans will "know what is the right
thing to do" from an ethical standpoint. Programs, workshops, and
seminars designed to educate these constituencies regarding the various dimensions and ethical aspects of athletics must be developed and
implemented. Many professions, including law and medicine, require
inservice training on a regular basis. While there are many programs
designed to teach coaches, administrators, athletes, and parents the
strategic or technical aspects of sport, few programs are designed to
develop knowledge and skills in the areas of ethics, sportsmanship,
and character.

4. *Development of Penalty Structure.* If a sports organization, league, or program wants to change the behavior of its coaches, athletes, or fans,
there must be clearly defined consequences for failure to act appropri-
ately. If, for example, an athlete or coach acts in an unsportsmanlike
manner, he or she should be penalized accordingly, whether within
the game itself or with ejection or a prolonged suspension. Fans must
understand that unsportsmanlike behavior will not be tolerated. It
must be clear that they will be removed from the premises if they do
not behave in a manner that is respectful of opponents. The punish-
ment for unethical or unsportsmanlike behavior must be clear, swift,
and certain.

5. *Evaluate the Program.* Once an athletic organization's educational efforts
and programs are in place, they must be evaluated to determine their
effectiveness in promoting positive ethical behavior. Evaluative tech-
niques range from observing behavior changes to actual cognitive pen-
and-pencil measures. Much literature is available about this cognitive

process (Beller, 1990; Beller & Stoll, 1992, 1995, 1996; Beller, Stoll, Burwell, & Cole, 1996; Bredemeier, 1984; Bredemeier & Shields, 1986; Hahm, 1989; Hall, 1981; Krause & Priest, 1993; Penny & Priest, 1990; Stoll, Beller, Cole, & Burwell, 1995; Wandzilak, Carroll, & Ansorge, 1988). If moral reasoning can be cognitively taught, then it can be evaluated. The charge is to find an instrument or technique to measure the effectiveness of the program in meeting its stated goals.

6. *Be a Good Role Model.* Finally, if we expect our athletic programs to promote ethical behavior and good sportsmanship, each and every one of us has a responsibility to be a positive role model. It is not enough to simply talk about ethics and good sportsmanship; our actions, day in and day out, must reflect our commitment to those principles.

If our athletic programs are to contribute positively to the ethical and moral development of athletes, they must be structured to do so. Our priorities must be clear, our commitment strong. Accomplishing this goal is neither simple nor simplistic, but rather requires courage and dedication to educational principles and programs that are multifaceted and multidimensional, involving coaches, administrators, athletes, students, fans, and the media.

As former athletes and coaches, we believe that sport has the potential to build moral character. To do so, however, would require a vastly different coaching methodology and participation environment. Specifically, we must reconsider how the win-at-all-costs attitude that permeates virtually every aspect of our athletic programs affects the moral and character development of participants. While teaching the will to win does not have to be eliminated, coaches, athletic administrators, and others in sport leadership positions must re-evaluate their philosophy regarding the importance of winning as it relates to character development, particularly when the participants are children and young adults. Without this fundamental shift in philosophy, sport will never fulfill its potential as a tool to educate and build positive character traits in our nation's youth.

REFERENCES

Allison, M. T. (1981). Sportsmanship: Variation on sex and degree of competitive experience. In A. Dunleavy, A. Miracle, & C. Rees (Eds.), *Studies in the sociology of sport* (pp. 153–165). Fort Worth: Texas Christian University Press.

Beller, J. M. (1990). *A moral reasoning intervention program for Division I athletes: Can athletes learn not to cheat?* Unpublished doctoral dissertation, University of Idaho, Moscow.

Beller, J. M., & Stoll, S. K. (1992, Spring). A moral reasoning intervention program for division I student-athletes. *Academic Athletic Journal*, pp. 43–57.

Beller, J. M., & Stoll, S. K. (1993a). High school through elite level athletes' moral reasoning. *Abstracts of Research Papers*, American Alliance for Health, Physical Education, Recreation, and Dance.

Beller, J. M., & Stoll, S. K., (1993b, August). Sportsmanship: An antiquated concept? *Journal of Physical Education, Recreation, and Dance*, pp. 74–79.

Beller, J. M., & Stoll, S. K. (1994, March). Sport participation and its effect on moral reasoning of high school student athletes and general students [Abstract]. *Research Quarterly for Exercise and Sport (Supplement), 65*, A-94.

Beller, J. M., & Stoll, S. K. (1995, November). Moral development of high school athletes. *Journal of Pediatric Exercise, 7*(4), 352–363.

Beller, J. M, Stoll, S. K., Burwell, B., & Cole, J. (1996, September). The relationship of competition and a Christian liberal arts education on moral reasoning of college student athletes. *Research on Christian Higher Education, 3*, 99–114.

Beller, J. M., Stoll, S. K., & Rudd, A. (1997). The great character debate [Abstract]. *Research Quarterly for Exercise and Sport, 68*(1), A-72.

Boyver, E. L. (1963). Children's concepts of sportsmanship in the fourth, fifth, and sixth grades. *Research Quarterly for Exercise and Sport, 34*, 282–287.

Bredemeier, B. J. (1984). Sport, gender, and moral growth. In J. M. Silva & R. S. Weinberg (Eds.), *Psychological foundations of sport* (pp. 400–413). Champaign, IL: Human Kinetics Press.

Bredemeier, B. J., & Shields, D. (1984). Divergence in moral reasoning about sport and life. *Sociology of Sport Journal, 1*, 348–357.

Bredemeier, B. J., & Shields, D. (1986). Moral growth among athletes and nonathletes: A comparative analysis. *Journal of Genetic Psychology, 147*(1), 7–18.

California State University Fullerton Department of HPERD. (1994). [Moral reasoning of division I male and female athletes]. Unpublished raw data.

Carrodine, K. (1993). [Moral reasoning of division I athletes]. Unpublished raw data.

Dubois, P. (1986). The effect of participation in sport on the value orientations of youth athletes. *Sociology of Sport Journal, 3*, 29–42.

Frankena, W. E. (1973). *Ethics* (2nd ed.). Englewood Cliffs, NJ: Prentice-Hall.

Gough, R. (1993). Writer questions ETHICS* research. *NCAA News, 30*(19), 4.

Hahm, C. H. (1989). *Moral reasoning and moral development among general students, physical education majors, and student athletes*. Unpublished doctoral dissertation, University of Idaho, Moscow.

Hahm, C. H., Beller, J. M., & Stoll, S. K. (1989). *The Hahm–Beller Values Choice Inventory*. (Available from J. Beller, Room 400 Memorial Gym, University of Idaho, Moscow, ID 83844)

Hall, E. (1981). *Moral development levels of athletes in sport specific and general social situations*. Unpublished doctoral dissertation, Texas Women's University.

Hansen, D. E., Beller, J. M., & Stoll, S. K. (1998). A comparison of moral reasoning scores between ninth grade student athletes and non-athletes. *Research Quarterly for Exercise and Sport, 69*(Suppl. 1), 122.

Kistler, J. W. (1957). Attitude expressed about behavior demonstrated in certain specific situations occurring in sport. *Annual Proceedings of the National College Physical Education Association, 60,* 55–58.

Kohlberg, L. (1981). *Essays on Moral Development: Vol. 1. The philosophy of moral development.* San Francisco: Harper & Row.

Krause, J., & Priest, B. (1993). *Longitudinal study of United States Military Academy cadets' moral reasoning (1988–92).* Unpublished manuscript, United States Military Academy, West Point.

Kretchmar, J. L. (1993). *A study on the moral judgements of intercollegiate student-athletes in sport situations.* Unpublished baccalaureate scholars thesis, Pennsylvania State University.

Kretchmar, R. S. (1994). *Practical philosophy of sport.* Champaign, IL: Human Kinetics Press.

Kroll, W. (1975, April). *Psychology of sportsmanship.* Paper presented at the Sport Psychology Meeting, NASPE, Atlantic City, NJ.

Kroll, W., & Petersen, K. H. (1965). Study of values test and collegiate football teams. *Research Quarterly, 36*(4), 441–447.

Lakie, W. L. (1964). Expressed attitudes of various groups of athletes toward athletic competition. *Research Quarterly for Exercise and Sport, 35,* 497–503.

Lickona, T. (1991). *Educating for character.* New York: Bantam Books.

Lumpkin, A., Stoll, S. K., & Beller, J. M. (1994). *Sport ethics: Applications for fair play.* St. Louis: CV Mosby.

Mangan, J. A. (1981). *Athleticism in the Victorian and Edwardian Public School.* London: Cambridge University Press.

McGinnis, A. (1993, May). Ethics is taught [Letter to the editor]. *NCAA News, 30*(14), 4.

Nelson, S. (1993). [Moral reasoning of male and female athletes at traditionally Seventh Day Adventist colleges]. Unpublished raw data.

Olgilvie, B., & Tutko, T. (1971). If you want to build character, try something else. *Psychology Today, 5,* 60.

Penny, B., & Priest, B. (1990). *Study of United States Military Academy cadets' moral reasoning.* Unpublished manuscript, United States Military Academy, West Point.

Rest, J. R. (1979). *The defining issues test.* (Available from the author, 330 Burton Hall, University of Minnesota, Minneapolis, MN 55455)

Rest, J. R. (1986). *Moral development: Advances in research and theory.* New York: Praeger.

Richardson, D. E. (1982). Ethical conduct in sport situations. *Annual Proceedings of the National College Physical Education Association, 66,* 98–104.

Sage, G. H. (1988, October). Sports participation as a builder of character. *The World and I,* pp. 629–641.

Sereny, G. (1996). *Albert Speer: His battle with the truth.* London: Picador.

Shields, D. L., & Bredemeier, B. J. (1995). *Character development and physical activity.* Champaign, IL: Human Kinetics Press.

Stoll, S. K., & Beller, J. M. (1989, Spring). A new moral value inventory: The Hahm–Beller value choice inventory. *IAHPERD Journal,* pp. 12–15.

Stoll, S. K., & Beller, J. M. (1991). [Moral reasoning of intercollegiate athletes, Part II]. Unpublished raw data.

Stoll, S. K., & Beller, J. M. (1992). [Moral reasoning of Olympic level male and
    female athletes]. Unpublished manuscript, University of Idaho, Moscow.

Stoll, S. K., & Beller, J. M. (1993, March). Effect of a longitudinal teaching method-
    ology and classroom environment on both cognitive and behavioral moral
    development [Abstract]. *Research Quarterly for Exercise and Sport (Supplement)*,
    64, A-112.

Stoll, S. K., & Beller, J. M. (1995, September). *The importance of teaching methodology
    in moral education of sport populations*. (ERIC Data Base, Resources in Educa-
    tion, No. ED 382 619)

Stoll, S. K., Beller, J. M., Cole, J., & Burwell, B. (1995, March). A comparison of
    moral reasoning scores of general students and student athletes in Division
    I and Division III NCAA member institutions [Abstract]. *Research Quarterly
    for Exercise and Sport (Supplement)*, *66*, A-81.

Wadilow, M. (1994). [Longitudinal study of United States Air Force Cadets' moral
    reasoning]. Unpublished data. United States Air Force Academy, Office of
    Research and Development, Colorado Springs.

Wandzilak, T., Carroll, T., & Ansorge, C. J. (1988). Values development through
    physical activity; Promoting sportsmanlike behaviors, perceptions, and moral
    reasoning. *Journal of Teaching in Physical Education*, *8*(1), 13–22.

3

Role Model: A Critical Assessment of the Application of the Term to Athletes

Todd W. Crosset

Twice an All-American on the University of San Francisco basketball team that won 55 straight games and two NCAA Championships, a member of the gold-medal-winning Olympic team in 1956, and center on the fabled Boston Celtic teams that won 11 NBA championships in 13 years, Bill Russell is one of the most successful athletes of our time. Despite such success, he often was criticized by fans and the media because he refused to sign autographs. One of his reasons for not doing so was that he saw no connection between his basketball ability and the expectation of fans that he be a "role model" for their children.

> During my career, people would come up to me and say, "Great Game, Bill. I want my son here to grow up to be just like you," he wrote in *Second Wind: The Memoirs of an Opinionated Man* (Russell & Branch, 1979). "I began to wonder. Those people didn't know a thing about me personally; for all they know, I might be a child molester. Yet, here were parents saying they wanted to model their children after me, instead of after themselves. I began to cringe at those comments; instead of flattering me, they made me sad. Over the years, I would learn better than anyone that my basketball skills and my parental ones were very different qualities." (p. 102)

One of our society's most widely accepted beliefs and a primary justification for our tremendous investment in sport, is that athletes are role models: shapers of youth and leaders in social change campaigns. The point of this chapter is to question the logic of this commonly held assumption.

This is not to suggest that there are no role models. Undoubtedly, parents, relatives, and nonrelated adults such as teachers or coaches often have a significant impact on young people (Scales & Gibbons, 1996). Nor is this to suggest that participation in athletics cannot mold character. Athletic programs, if conducted in a way that emphasizes the value of the process (participation) as opposed to the outcome (winning), can instill in participants an appreciation for hard work, honesty, teamwork, and discipline. Learning these valuable traits through actual participation, however, is an entirely different matter than expecting the character traits displayed on the fields of play to be transferred to the fan or, more specifically, a youngster, simply by watching athletes on television or reading about them in the newspaper.

DEFINING A ROLE MODEL

Very few social scientists use the term "role model." Most observers of human behavior do not find it a useful concept to explain why people make certain life choices (Jung, 1986). Those few who do use the term are most likely researchers interested in youth and education. People identified as role models are generally adults with whom youngsters have daily to monthly contact. Technically, role models are "nonparental, significant adults or extended family members" (Galbo & Demetrulias, 1996; Scales & Gibbons, 1996). Role models are not God-like or transcendent beings, but rather the "regular" people in our everyday lives who provide guidance and upon whom we model our behavior (Porpora, 1996).

Based on this definition, athletes would not, in fact, cannot, be role models. Athletes, at least from the fan's perspective, are high-status, non-related adults with whom the observer has little personal contact. Inherent in the belief that athletes are role models is the assumption that a leap can be made from being an admired public figure to having a very direct and personal influence on a young person's behavior. As with many of the myths we accept regarding sport, an athlete's impact as a role model is largely assumed. While it is clear that millions of people admire athletes, it is impossible to determine the impact of this admiration on behavior. People can name public figures and celebrities they admire, but to make a connection between admiration and a direct effect on personal behavior is a stretch. Even if such a connection could be measured, it is likely that a big-time athlete's influence on young people's behavior is overstated (Jung, 1986).

Does John Elway, for example, simply by virtue of his position as an admired sports figure, cause significant change in fans' beliefs and values? Do youngsters change their everyday behavior as a result of what they have seen or heard about him? Except in the most extreme cases, the answer is no.

Young people may model a batting stance or a jump shot after a sports figure. But to expect or even suggest that admiration for an athlete's ability to run fast or jump high will cause someone to change his or her personal behavior, values, or beliefs in meaningful and long-lasting ways is misguided. While an athlete's visit to a hospital ward to cheer a child stricken with cancer may brighten that child's outlook, it is highly unlikely that a one-time visit will alter the child's personal behavior. Despite what parents, coaches, athletic administrators, and athletes themselves might think, an athlete's ability to affect behavior is limited almost entirely to specific, on-the-field or court athletic actions and attitudes. In short, the common belief that athletes are role models has been blown wildly out of proportion.

Why then have we come to unquestioningly accept the notion that athletes influence personal behavior of people they have virtually no direct contact with—that they are "role models"? While there are many factors that could affect the widespread acceptance of any societal belief, for purposes of this discussion, the following four will be examined:

1. A shift in the process by which people become famous
2. Shifts in family life resulting in an increased concern for the welfare of children
3. "Reciprocity" in sport
4. The desire to control the behavior of athletes, particularly Black male athletes

ANDY WARHOL WAS CORRECT

Key to the discussion of the popularity of the term "role model" is understanding how the process of becoming famous has shifted. Role model gained currency in popular culture at about the same time heroes were replaced by celebrities as our cultural icons. Thus, role model is a compensatory concept, a weak substitute for our loss of heroes.

Heroes exhibit supernatural, God-like qualities, displaying for us an ideal. While heroes inspire us to be better, we never imagine ourselves attaining a similar level of greatness. Rather, we try to adopt the heroes' best qualities as our own. Heroes personify transcendent ideals and transcendent visions of the good (Porpora, 1996). Scholars draw a sharp distinction between heroes and celebrities. The former are worth admiring because they are almost certainly better than we are. Celebrities, however, are not necessarily better; they are simply better known.

A hero's fame is perceived as being earned and, thus, deserved, based on a high quality of achievement. American heroes from the first third of the twentieth century, like Babe Ruth, Red Grange, Sonja Henie, and Helen Wills, deserved the attention they received. Their accomplishments were truly heroic. This is not to suggest that some publicity apparatus did not help to frame and publicize their heroic deeds (Gamson, 1994). What would Ruth have been without his ghost writer Christy Walsh, Grange without Pyle, or the whole lot without the "Gee Wiz" reporting of the 1920s. Because the publicity apparatus remained, for the most part, hidden from view during this "Golden Age of Sport," the public did not wonder whether the fame and glory heaped on athletes was deserved.

The difficulty in trying to be a hero today is that the distance from the public necessary to achieve and maintain heroic stature no longer exists. When Ruth tore through the press car naked, followed by a naked, knife-wielding woman, no reporter dared write about the incident. Today, such a story would not only get printed, but no doubt land Ruth and the woman on the talk show circuit and result in a book contract and made-for-TV movie deal. Information about the everyday life of the famous is in high demand. Maintaining the distance necessary to be heroic (God-like) is no longer possible.

Fame is not tied to quality of achievement. One can be famous simply because one is known; that is, a celebrity. The public admires today's celebrities not for their accomplishments, but for their interesting exploits. Madonna, Evel Knievel, and Hulk Hogan, for example, are all admired for their ability to maintain interest. This is what Gamson (1994) refers to as audiences' operational aesthetic: an appreciation of the process of holding the publicity apparatus' gaze, or the art of staying in the public eye.

Apparently, Andy Warhol's prediction that everyone would enjoy 15 minutes of fame has become reality. The editors of *People* magazine, by their own admission, shine their spotlight on ordinary folks for a fleeting experience of fame, which soon fades, as these subjects return to a life of quiet obscurity.

If a hero is known for achievement and reveals the potential of humanity, the celebrity is known for well-knownness and reveals the possibility of the press and media. To be famous today, it is not nearly as important to be newsworthy as it is to know how to get into the news. As a consequence, the hero, dependent on achievement and transcendent qualities cultivated through distance, has all but disappeared from American society.

Whether it is the overexposure of public figures, the market appeal of celebrities, or a new sophisticated audience, the point is the same: how people get to be famous has changed. The publicity industry is now center stage. Consequently, it is the celebrity who has come to replace the hero in our culture.

Regrettably, celebrities do not inspire us to be our best. We may like to follow and discuss their accomplishments and personal lives, but we are not about to hoist celebrities up as moral exemplars. With the demise of heroes, with their transcendent qualities, and the rise of the celebrity, representing fame devoid of achievement, on some level we fear that we have lost the credible, mythic figures that help shape social behavior. When potential heroes are reduced to celebrities, we fill the void with role models. Like heroes, role models are worth admiring, but not necessarily because they are better than us. "That is, apparently, the utility of [role models] that it is no great trick to emulate them" (Aristides, 1991, p. 329). We pull our role models from our everyday lives. While they may not inspire us, they can guide us in right action.

HELP RAISE OUR CHILDREN . . . PLEASE!

While it may be understandable why the role model gained currency in our culture, why was it applied to those outside our immediate families and neighborhoods? Role model as it currently is applied to athletes is a product of a society that views its children as being "at risk."

In many ways, our children are at risk. One in five children is raised in poverty. We live in a society in which parents find it increasingly difficult to spend time with their children, where the cost of living is so high that both parents are forced to work, where most men continue to view parenting as an option rather than a shared responsibility. We live in a society of gated communities filled with independent families whose ties and obligations seem to extend only to those with whom they share living space. Children in poverty, dysfunctional families, broken homes, latchkey kids—all contribute to the perception that children need more guidance than normally can be provided by parents, relatives, and teachers.

But the real risks children face are heightened by an overemphasis on traditional family units. The attachment to the single-breadwinner, two-parent, stable family is quite strong in American culture. But the reality is that only 7% of families live up to this ideal (Giddens, 1991). A substantial number of children live in single-parent households or in stepfamilies. While it is doubtful that these nontraditional family structures have a long-term negative impact on children, the problems of society often are attributed to the "breakdown of the family."

Without heroes to inspire them and full-time parents to guide them, combined with the perception that the family is breaking down, children are viewed as a social problem. As a result, we believe that we need people to hold up as positive examples for children. Without these role models, we believe that our young people are at risk of losing their moral bearings. In such a world, the notion that athletes could be role models for our children is a very seductive, if not hopeful, concept in the context of these rather difficult times.

But why athletes?

ATHLETES "OWE US"

Americans repeatedly have called on sport and its athletes to help cure perceived social ills. At the turn of the twentieth century we called on sport to civilize immigrants, in the 1950s and 1960s sport was a political weapon in the cold war, and in the 1970s we implored kids to get high on sports rather than drugs. Now we are asking athletes to socialize young spectators.

Why do we ask so much from sports and the athletes who play them? We do not ask as much from other highly visible entertainers. Admission of wife battery or drug use by a Hollywood star, for example, does not get the same response as a similar admission by an athlete. It is safe to say that most parents would prefer that their children model their behavior after Shaquille O'Neal the basketball player rather than Shaquille O'Neal the rap artist. The answer lies in part in the relationship between the fan and the sporting event.

Sport does not play to the audience. Players are not trying to increase drama for the pleasure of the fans; rather, they are trying to win the game. For proof, one need look no further than the Super Bowl, notorious for not being a very entertaining game—a game without drama. If sport were like other forms of entertainment, the players would be sure to put on a great show on their biggest night of the year. If athletes do not attempt to effect an emotional response in the audience, what makes sport such an appealing form of entertainment?

Part of the appeal of sport is that the audience believes (and rightly so) that it can have an effect on the emotional state of the players and thus impact the final result. A number of academic papers suggest that home field is an advantage (Leifer, 1995). In short, fan support matters.

Of course, fans sometimes hold an exaggerated view of their impact. In any local sports bar during the "Game of the Century," fans undoubtedly will be seen engaging in rituals that suggest they have telepathic powers. Some fans will switch a lucky ball to their other hand if their team is losing. Others will begin watching a different set. As humorous as this seems, it illustrates the extent to which fans believe they make a tangible contribution to their team's effort to win.

The fan–athlete relationship lies, at least in part, outside the system of rational exchange and within a system of reciprocity—or gift giving. The athlete gives the fan the gift of superior performance. Fans are moved by these displays and demonstrate that they appreciate the gift by attending events, wearing logo-laden clothing, and honoring athletes with testimonials and parades.

Sociologists have studied the norms associated with Christmas gift giving (Caplow, 1984), blood donations (Titmus, 1971), and material and emotional giving between spouses (Hochshield, 1989). These studies support the notion of universal norms of reciprocity (Gouldner, 1960). One norm of reciprocity is that a gift establishes a feeling-bond between two people, while the sale of a commodity does not necessarily leave a connection (Hyde, 1983). We feel tied to those who give us gifts in a way that would seem unthinkable had we purchased the same object from them. This feeling may account for some of the passion fans demonstrate for their teams.

Another norm of reciprocity systems is the circularity of giving— what goes around comes around. Clearly, applause has a dual purpose. It is a sign of appreciation for the gift of an excellent or moving performance and, at the same time, it is a gift given in return. There is a certain thrill in knowing that your gift, your talent, was received and appreciated. Thus, fans shower applause and support on athletes in an attempt to help them play at a "higher" level.

As a result of the expectation of the gift "coming back around," fans believe that athletes are obligated to them and the community that supports the athletes. In sports that depend on city or regional identity, the expectation that athletes will give back to the community is high. And the most obvious, and seemingly simplest, way that athletes can give back to the community is to be positive role models for the community's children.

THE ROLE MODEL AS A "CREDIT TO HIS RACE"

The term "role model" has been applied to many types of athletes. A cursory review of the application of the term to athletes in the popular media reveals that it is disproportionally applied to women and African-American athletes. This disproportionality is not unique to sports. Jung (1986) has noted that "one rarely hears of a successful majority group member being exalted as a role model for his/her own majority group.

It is implicitly recognized that majority group members don't need role models to the same extent as minorities" (p. 534). For example, when Warren Moon, an African-American quarterback, was accused of wife abuse, many lamented the loss of a role model. At about the same time, Bobby Cox, the White manager of the Atlanta Braves, faced similar charges. Few, however, worried whether Cox's actions would adversely affect children.

Do Black athletes make better role models? Do Black athletes owe more to the community than White athletes? Probably not. But the phrase is applied so frequently to Black athletes that at least one scholar has suggested that "role model" is a racially coded term (Shropshire, 1996).

Racially coded terms are phrases that conjure up racial stereotypes without directly alluding to race. For example, "welfare queen" and "All-American" are racially coded. The former evokes images of Black women, and the latter, of White men. The frequency with which role model is applied to Black athletes and the likelihood that it is racially coded suggest that we need to understand the appeal of the term within a racial context.

The use of role model coincides with the dramatic increase of African-Americans in "prime time" sports following the civil rights movement. Black athletes have been portrayed, primarily by White society, as positive examples for Black youth. Indeed, White commentators seem almost pathologically obsessed with Black athletes' behavior and influence on Black youth. I suspect this has less to do with concern for Black youth than it does with the desire to placate the fears of predominantly White audiences. Could it be that insistence upon athletes being role models is also a way of controlling the behavior of a group of highly visible Black men—to subtly encourage them to act in a nonthreatening way?

Fear of Black youth is deeply felt in the White community. Young Black men continue to be routinely questioned by the police, followed by security guards, and generally viewed with suspicion. Black athletes, commentators, and image consultants work to reduce fears by portraying Black men as nonthreatening. From Joe Louis to Jackie Robinson to Grant Hill and Tiger Woods, the images of Black athletes have been framed so as to reduce fears of Whites. Could it be that we do not want Black athletes to upset the All-American, puritan, White image of sport?

When athletes of color (and adolescent athletes) do step out of line, they are quickly reminded of their obligations as athletes—to be role models. And when Black athletes resist the imposition of role-model status, as Russell, Jim Brown, and Charles Barkley have, they are roundly criticized. This public outcry for Black athletes to be role models is a way of encouraging them to behave in accordance with the expectations of the majority. We expect them to express and display the dominant ideals, support the status quo, and not question the authority of owners, coaches, and league officials. The application of role-model status and the resultant expectations it entails are not simply about a concern for children—they are about maintaining social control.

African-American youth, not surprisingly, can see through the hype. One study, funded by the Robert Wood Johnson Foundation, concluded that "inner city teens would be delighted to meet their favorite NBA star, if he came to their school to speak against drugs. But they would discount the appearance as 'playing the game'—performing one of the obligations of being a celebrity. They would feel he had little to tell them about their lives. To be effective, a spokesperson would have to possess a 'reputation' within this community" (MEE Report, 1992, p. viii).

The racial disparity in the use of the term also says something about the dominant explanation for the persistence of racial inequality. According to this view, marginalized groups remain behind because of a lack of technical or social know-how. Role models, pioneers, and path breakers from marginalized groups, it is assumed, will be an inspiration for others who share a similar identity. This commonly held perspective assumes that overt racism has ended and the persistence of inequality is merely a cultural lag.

There are two problems with this view. First, it hides the real reason for inequality—discrimination. The reality is that inequalities persist due to a sedimentation of the impact of racism and the continued racist practices of Whites. Second, it distorts the real impact of path breakers of color on organizations. Integrating people of color into an organization has a significant impact on other people in that organization. The success of people of color in some organizations probably has less to do with inspiration of role models and more to do with organizations changing to become more inclusive. Despite these flaws in logic, the racial disparity in the use of role model persists, in part, because it helps to calm White fears and fits an explanation of racial inequality that has limited costs for Whites. As such, it is not too far afield to suggest that role model as it is often applied to Black athletes is a subtle form of racism.

ATHLETES ARE NOT THE SOLUTION

While the above reasons help explain our expectation that athletes be positive role models, one fundamental problem remains. Athletes do not make very good role models.

An effective role model must have considerable, direct, and consistent contact with the young people for whom he or she wishes to provide an example. The very nature of being a highly successful athlete prohibits such frequent interaction. Athletics, as those who participate on the elite level will attest, is incredibly time-consuming. Athletic success demands such a single-mindedness of purpose that the athlete does not have the time to be an effective role model.

The competing demands of being an excellent athlete and a role model result in some serious hypocrisy. A glaring example of athlete-as-less-than-effective-role model is the National Basketball Association's "Stay in School" program. Asking a group of athletes, a large percentage of whom have made a choice not to complete their schooling to participate in this program is misguided at best and hypocritical at worst. While the effort is well-intentioned, the words simply ring hollow. Forcing athletes into this public position undermines their credibility and insults the public's intelligence. Simply being able to run fast or jump high does not make someone a good role model. There is nothing to suggest that highly successful athletes are any better equipped to be positive role models than are teachers or neighbors.

Undoubtedly, athletes should be expected to give back to the community that supports them so well. So too, for that matter, should all citizens, regardless of race, occupation, or social status. But setting athletes up as more important role models or expecting them to accept a larger share of the responsibility for raising our children is not only unwise, it is unfair. The athlete-as-role model is a poor alternative to real intervention in children's lives—intervention by people who are in a far better position to directly and consistently influence children. It is unreasonable to ask someone who is neither equipped nor has the time or inclination to do so, to be responsible for raising our children simply because he or she is physically skilled. We will be far more successful in shaping young people in and out of athletics when our social agenda pressures the state and corporations to support increased adult–youth interaction and when we provide parents the resources to reclaim their obligation to intervene in children's lives directly and consistently.

We must be realistic about what we expect of our athletes. More specifically, we must let go of our idealized notion of the athlete as a role model. We cannot continue to expect celebrity athletes to pick up the slack for overworked parents. Nor should we ask athletes, by virtue of their physical prowess, to be leaders in resolving social conflict or effective in ending racial hostility. The only thing more disturbing than athletes who we feel do not live up to our expectations of them as role models, is the fact that we have chosen them, rather than ourselves, as the people who are best equipped to address our social problems.

REFERENCES

Aristides. (1991). Knocking on three, Winston. *American Scholar,* pp. 327–336.

Caplow, T. (1984). Rule enforcement without visible means: Christmas gift giving in Middletown. *American Journal of Sociology, 89*(6), 1306–1323.

Galbo, J. J., & Demetrulias, D. M. (1996). Recollection of nonparental significant adults during childhood and adolescence. *Youth and Society, 27*(4), 403–420.

Gamson, J. (1994). *Claims to fame: Celebrity in contemporary America.* Berkeley: University of California Press.

Giddens, A. (1991). *Introduction to sociology.* New York: Norton.

Gouldner, A. W. (1960). The norms of reciprocity: A preliminary statement. *American Sociological Review, 25*(2), 161–178.

Hochshield, A. R. (1989). The economy of gratitude. In D. D. Franks & E. D. McCarty (Eds.), *The sociology of emotions: Original essays and research papers* (pp. 95–114). Greenwich, CT: JAI Press.

Hyde, L. (1983). *The Gift: Imagination and the erotic life of property.* New York, Vintage Books.

Jung, J. (1986). How useful is the concept of role model? A critical analysis. *Journal of Social Behavior and Personality, 1*(4), 525–536.

Leifer, E. (1995). *Making the majors: The transformation of team sports in America.* Cambridge, MA: Harvard University Press.

Porpora, D. V. (1996). Personal heroes, religion and transcendental metanarratives. *Sociological Forum, 11*(2), 209–229.

Russell, B., & Branch, T. (1979). *Second wind: The memoirs of an opinionated man.* New York: Random House.

Scales, P. C., & Gibbons, J. L. (1996). Extended family members and unrelated adults in the lives of young adolescents: A research agenda. *Journal of Early Adolescence, 16*(4), 365–389.

Shropshire, K. L. (1996, November). Role models, sport, race and the law. Presentation at meeting of the North American Society for the Sociology of Sport, Birmingham.

The MEE Report: Researching the Hip-Hop Generation. (1992). Research Division of MEE Productions, Inc. for the Robert Wood Johnson Foundation, I. D. 18762.

Titmus, R. M. (1971). *The gift relationship: From human blood to social policy.* New York: Random House.

4

College Athletics as Good Business?

John R. Gerdy

Concern regarding making ends meet financially has been as much a part of the history of American higher education as the classroom lecture. Contrary to prevailing notions about sport's ability to contribute to the well-balanced education of student-athletes, it was the never-ending search for new revenue streams that was the driving force behind the formal incorporation of athletics into higher education. As public interest in college football grew in the late nineteenth and early twentieth century, leaders of financially strapped colleges and universities saw athletics as a means to generate much-needed resources in the form of money and visibility.

> While the need for resources has remained an ever-pressing imperative throughout the history of higher education in this country, it was only at the turn of the century, with the invention of mass sports in America and the complex of factors that affected the university's internal and external constituencies, that resource acquisition through athletics became a possibility. A sports-hungry populace consumed athletic entertainment with increasing gusto as the tempo of industrialization, urbanization, leisure time, and accumulation of expendable capital quickened. The large land-grant schools saw a means of acquiring increased support from the legislature and the people. Representing the community, each school's victory provided it with rights to boast to the people of its state. Through each victory, the often culturally diffuse and geographically disparate peoples of the region could be unified. (Chu, 1989, pp. 33–34)

Regardless of whether a successful sports team generated additional resources and political favor for a university— points that remain in dispute to this day—college presidents *believed* that a successful football pro-

Portions of this chapter were taken from the author's work entitled *The successful college athletic program: The new standard.* (1997). Phoenix, AZ: American Council on Education/Oryx Press.

gram legitimized their institution as a major university. Athletics was formally incorporated into higher education's structure because academic leaders believed that a successful athletic team could serve an important public relations function for the university, which, in turn, would result in increased financial support. This, along with the alleged "educational benefits" that accrued to participants, made the marriage of athletics and higher education seem reasonable. From these beginnings, this belief has evolved to the point where it is now accepted as an unchallenged "truth."

With coaches signing six-figure contracts, 100,000-seat football stadiums sold out, CBS paying a staggering $6 *billion* for the right to televise the NCAA men's basketball tournament for 11 years, and institutions receiving $5 million or more for participating in a football bowl game, it is no wonder many think college athletic programs are rolling in the dough. Coupled with the occasional report of an athletic department writing a $100,000 check to the institution's library to purchase books, it is understandable that the public believes that athletic departments not only generate a huge financial surplus, but direct a portion of that surplus to the institution's general education budget. Even athletic departments that operate at a deficit purportedly contribute to the educational mission of the university in the form of exposure generated through the media, particularly television. Such exposure enhances the institution's stature and generates public interest in the university, resulting in increased applications, alumni donations, and favor with legislators and the surrounding community.

The purpose of this chapter is to examine whether these assertions are true and whether athletics is a sound fiscal investment for a university.

THE MONEY-MAKING MYTH

If athletic programs were embraced by the higher education community largely for financial reasons, what type of fiscal returns are being realized on this investment? Unfortunately, not very good ones, according to virtually every analysis of the economics of college sports.

According to a biannual NCAA-sponsored report, *Revenues and Expenses of Intercollegiate Athletic Programs: Financial Trends and Relationships*, when institutional support (salaries, cash, tuition waivers, etc.) is not included on the revenue side of the financial ledger, most Division I college athletic programs lose money. For example, in 1993, only 30% of Division I programs that responded to a survey reported generating more revenue than they expended. Further, only 51% percent of the Division I-A schools that responded reported generating a profit. According to the 1995 report,

Table 4.1. Percentage of College Athletics Programs that Generated Profit,
Loss, or Broke Even (excluding institutional support) in 1993, 1995,
and 1997.

		Profit	*Deficit*	*Even*
Division I-A	1997	43%	56%	1%
	1995	46%	52%	2%
	1993	51%	49%	0%
Division I-AA	1997	9%	90%	1%
	1995	13%	85%	2%
	1993	15%	81%	5%
Division I-AAA	1997	10%	89%	1%
	1995	18%	82%	0%
	1993	17%	81%	2%

Source: Fulks, 1993, pp. 19, 33, 47; 1995, pp. 19, 33, 47; and 1997, pp. 20, 35, 50

the financial outlook was even more negative. That report revealed that
only 28% of the Division I programs that responded and only 46% of
Division I-A programs that responded reported generating a profit. This
downward financial trend continues as reflected in the NCAA's most recent report in 1997, which showed that only 22% of Division I programs
and far fewer than half (43%) of Division I-A programs reported generating a profit. Without general institutional support, less than one in four
Division I athletic programs would be solvent.

A more detailed accounting of the financial statistics from these reports is in Table 4.1.

Further, it is likely that the future financial outlook will be increasingly negative as institutions are being mandated to appropriate equal
athletic funding for women according to the provisions of Title IX of the
1972 Educational Amendment Act.

There is more to the issue of athletics as a sound institutional investment. The National Association of College and University Business Officers (NACUBO) conducted an analysis of college athletics' finances, as
reported in *The Financial Management of Intercollegiate Athletics Programs*
(1993). The analysis brought to light additional concerns regarding university accounting procedures as they applied to athletic operations. The
report concluded that current costs, as high as they are, may not be telling
the entire financial story. Specifically, the report questioned the practice

of institutions paying many indirect or overhead costs generated by the athletic department.

The report identified six sources of indirect expenditures.

- Amortization of facilities (if owned by the university)
- Student support services (academic and financial assistance) provided by the institution
- Student health services provided by the institution
- Athletics staff salaries and benefits for staff employed in other departments
- Proportion of buildings and grounds maintenance
- Proportion of capital equipment used

> Interviews with personnel in 18 institutions across all athletic divisions showed that only one of these data elements, amortization of facilities, could be calculated with any degree of accuracy, and even then this could be done only by the four Division I-A institutions in the study. Given this difficulty, it seems likely that many indirect or "overhead" expenses attributable to athletics activities are borne by the university as a whole. In institutions that require other programs or divisions to bear their share of indirect costs, allowing athletics to escape this burden creates a basic inequity. (NACUBO, 1993, p. 20)

Accordingly, we can easily conclude that were athletics' accounting held to a common business standard, where all direct and indirect expenses are charged against revenues, significantly fewer than 22% of Division I institutions would report an athletic department profit.

Inasmuch as athletics was formally incorporated into higher education primarily for financial and business reasons, it is ironic that this "business proposition" is usually a bad one. A successful business generates more money than it expends. Except for the very elite programs, rather than generating a positive revenue stream, athletics actually drains financial resources from the university.

> A review of the reports published over the past decade indicates that, as a whole, American intercollegiate athletics programs are unable to support themselves and that most programs run a deficit. This finding is not surprising in colleges that designate varsity sports as part of the educational budget and make no claim to seek massive crowds. It does warrant concern, however, when one looks at institutions that have established varsity football and/or basketball as major, self-supporting activities intended to produce revenues, with large arenas and stadia and with television audiences. (Thelin & Wiseman, 1989, p. 15)

The claim that athletic programs make money for the university is largely untrue. Yes, athletic programs *generate* revenue. Yes, occasionally we read about an athletic department writing a check to the university's general scholarship fund. What is not as readily reported, however, is that major college athletic programs spend a tremendous amount of money, particularly in the sports of football and basketball.

According to the NCAA's *Revenues and Expenses of Intercollegiate Athletic Programs: Financial Trends and Relationships,* in 1997, annual expenses for Division I-A football programs ranged from over $1.5 million to slightly less than $10 million. In 1995, 66% of schools reported a football budget ranging between $3.0 and $7.0 million. Men's basketball program expenses, although far less, are still significant, with budgets ranging from $200,000 to over $1.8 million. Fifty-one percent of basketball programs at Division I-A institutions reported expenses in excess of $1.0 million (the 1997 study did not report these frequency distributions). While many football and basketball programs operate at a profit, a sizable number do not. According to the 1997 report, 29% of Division I-A football programs and 81% of Division I-AA programs reported an operating deficit. The same study revealed that in men's basketball, 26% of programs at Division I-A institutions, 69% at Division I-AA institutions, and 61% at Division I-AAA institutions reported an operating deficit (Fulks, 1997). These numbers are significant, as football and basketball programs are alleged to generate a positive revenue flow, that helps pay for other sports, such as tennis, golf, and various women's sports. Contrary to popular belief, many football and basketball programs do not even pay for themselves.

Athletic directors and even college presidents often downplay these deficits, indicating that athletics consumes a very small percentage of the overall institutional budget. While the amount of institutional dollars spent on athletics may be small, the impact of this spending is great. Athletics is by far the largest and clearest window through which the public views the university. According to an NCAA-sponsored survey, 53% of the American public, 65% of men and 43% of women, follow college sports (National Collegiate Athletic Association, 1991, p. 22). "Of all the column inches written about the University, I would estimate that 75 percent is regarding the athletic program," Scott Selheimer, Director of Sports Information at the University of Delaware, told Bob Torpor in an interview in *Marketing Higher Education* (Torpor, 1995, p. 6). With such visibility comes increased public scrutiny. Spending on athletics reflects, at least in the public's eye, institutional priorities to a greater degree than any other university entity. If public opinion evolves to a point where the negatives associated with major college athletics (i.e., recruiting scandals, coaches being paid more than presidents, compromising of academic standards, etc.) cannot be rationalized away based on athletics' financial and institutional advancement benefits, universities will become even more hard-pressed to justify expensive athletic programs.

MORE MYTHS?

In most cases, the link between the athletic department and the institution in financial matters is weak. For example, many big-time athletic programs are run as independent, profit-driven, auxiliary enterprises. Despite the claim from athletic fund raisers that they work closely with the institutional advancement office to raise funds for the university, such cooperation is usually superficial. Because of the separation and mistrust that exist between most academic and athletic communities, virtually all athletic department fund-raising efforts are directed at raising money specifically for sports, rather than the institution generally. Money generated and raised by the athletic department is spent by the athletic department. It is rare when an athletic department donates money to the institution, because typically there is no excess revenue to donate. Even in those cases where an athletic department receives a financial windfall in the form of a bowl payout, much of the revenue is split among conference members, and what is left often is spent for the travel, lodging, and entertainment expenses of athletic department employees and "friends" who attend the game and the festivities that surround it.

Further, there is no conclusive evidence that a successful athletic program results in increased alumni giving or applications. The research simply does not support this assertion. For example, "in 1986, the year after Tulane shut down its basketball program in the wake of a point shaving scandal, donations to that school leapt by $5 million. Wichita State raised $26 million in a special drive in '87, the year in which it dropped football" (Wolff, 1995, p. 25). A successful athletic program can be a factor in alumni giving and student applications, but it is unlikely that it has much of a long-term effect. While an institution may experience an immediate, short-term jump in applications or financial support (more than likely earmarked specifically for the athletic program rather than the institution generally) after a particularly successful football or basketball season, most institutions will continue to attract quality students who, when they graduate, will donate money to their alma mater, with little regard to the quality or even existence of a highly competitive athletic program.

Major college athletic programs do, however, provide significant regional and national visibility for the school. Games are broadcast on radio and television to a national audience, and newspaper coverage is often extensive. "By 1900, the relationship between football and public relations had been firmly established and almost everywhere acknowledged as one of sport's major justifications" (Rudolph, 1990, p. 385). Clearly, athletic programs generate significant public exposure for universities. What is not so clear, however, is whether that exposure contributes positively to public relations.

A striking example of this dichotomy occurred at Florida State University. In winning a national football championship by defeating the University of Nebraska in the 1994 Orange Bowl, the university garnered a tremendous amount of positive publicity. A national championship in football was evidence of Florida State University's commitment to excellence. FSU was the best in the nation. FSU was a winner! There was no reason to expect that other programs offered by the university were of lesser quality.

How quickly things can change. Shortly after the Orange Bowl victory, allegations that student-athletes were provided clothes and cash by agents while coaches "looked the other way" quickly changed the type of exposure the football program was generating. If winning a national football championship translated into Florida State University being considered a winner, how did allegations that the football program won the national championship while breaking NCAA rules, translate?

Questions regarding the professed positive effect of athletic department visibility on the university go beyond the bad publicity associated with a scandal. Despite the claim that the athletic department generates visibility for the university generally, the exposure generated through athletics has very little to do with advancing positive educational or institutional messages. Such visibility is utilized simply to promote the specific goals of the athletic department.

To illustrate this point, the National Association of Athletics Compliance Coordinators (1995) conducted a study during the 1994–95 academic year in which observers were asked to distinguish the types of educational or athletic themes projected throughout the telecasts of various college football and basketball contests. Sixty-one surveys were completed charting 37 different NCAA basketball contests, and 111 surveys charting 42 different football telecasts. The study showed that only 13.2% of viewers rated the telecast as "effective" and less than 1% percent (.6%) as "very effective in informing [the viewer] about the universities, higher education or education generally." More than half (55.7%) indicated that the telecast charted was "not effective in promoting or highlighting an educational theme."

Television is not the only vehicle through which athletics interfaces with the public. Athletic events also are broadcast on radio networks and covered in local and national newspapers and magazines. Athletic departments produce an incredible amount of material promoting their teams, from media guides to game programs to posters. Athletic events themselves offer an opportunity to address a captive audience on campus. The images, messages, and themes associated with these productions, publications, and events, however, are almost exclusively athletic, with the incorporation of educational messages an afterthought at best.

Even the athletic scholarship, portrayed by coaches and athletic administrators as an educational opportunity, has very little to do with education. While coaches and athletic administrators claim that student-athletes' primary reason for being on campus is to earn a degree, the fact is they are recruited for entertainment purposes. This makes them the only student group recruited primarily for nonacademic purposes. Once they are on campus, it is made clear to them that athletics is their number one priority.

The review of the questionable positive financial impact of athletics on the university begs other questions. For example, while increasingly run as a profit-driven, business enterprise, the NCAA and its athletic departments are considered nonprofit entities. This suspect designation affects taxpayers, as the NCAA pays no state or federal taxes on the billions earned from television contracts, sponsorship deals, and licensing agreements. What does it say about institutional priorities when the basketball or football coach is paid three or four times what the president is paid? The high salaries received by coaches are justified on the basis that they are necessary to attract a top-notch coach to produce a winning team to generate money that eventually will be used for the benefit of the institution. While that sounds good, the fact is that for every coach who makes $500,000, there are five others who would do the job for much less, and probably do it just as well.

It is ironic that athletic directors justify these exorbitant compensation packages on the basis that they are competing in a high-stakes business, when such high compensation packages run contrary to the fundamental business principle of supply and demand. There are hundreds of quality coaches throughout the country who would jump at the opportunity to coach at the NCAA Division I level for a salary that is in line with that received by a senior faculty member rather than a Fortune 500 company executive.

EMPIRICAL DATA FOR HONEST DIALOGUE

My purpose is not to criticize unduly or to dismiss the positive impact an athletic program can have on a university, financially or otherwise. A well-run program can contribute to the mission of a university in ways that might not show up in the institutional balance sheet. Visibility and stature within the state legislature may, in some cases, have a positive impact on institutional efforts to attract state funding. Despite inconclusive evidence, a successful athletic team and the visibility it brings have the potential to attract students to campus, if not in the long run, certainly in the short run on an occasional basis.

However, given the financial statements and the inconclusive research regarding alumni giving and applications, coaches and athletic administrators no longer can assert without question that athletics is a positive financial proposition for the institution. Most athletic departments lose money. The claim that athletics has a major, long-term impact on student applications is suspect at best. The exposure generated through athletics does very little to promote the broad goals and programs of the university, but rather serves to promote the specific purposes of the athletic department. What's worse, not all of the visibility that athletics brings to the university is positive. Ask any president of a school that has been placed on NCAA probation. In short, athletic departments are run more as an entertainment enterprise catering to external constituencies (alumni, fans, and television networks) and thus are driven by market forces rather than educational priorities.

There is nothing inherently wrong with justifying athletic departments based on their financial impact on the institution. Nor is there anything evil in the fact that athletic departments are run as business propositions. Universities have long operated profit-driven auxiliary enterprises, bookstores and real estate development ventures being prime examples. And it is certainly not unusual that a university department fails to operate in the black. What is troublesome, however, is that in evaluating athletics' role on campus, we continue to base our discussion on myths, half-truths, hopeful claims, and antecdotal accounts rather than on empirical data and solid research.

As we enter the new millennium, all university departments are being challenged to justify how effective they are in contributing to the goals and mission of the institution. While athletics is certainly popular with the public, it is not so popular that we can afford not to hold it to the same level of scrutiny as other university enterprises. The effectiveness with which athletic programs contribute to the mission of our colleges and universities and the effect of such programs on our nation's educational efforts must be discussed openly and evaluated honestly. Despite media reports of athletic departments awash in money, the positive financial and institutional advancement impact of athletic programs on colleges and universities is overstated. Only when we acknowledge this reality will we be able to engage in meaningful dialogue regarding the proper role of athletics in American higher education.

REFERENCES

Chu, D. (1989). *The character of American higher education and intercollegiate sport.* Albany: State University of New York Press.

Fulks, D. L. (1993). *Revenues and expenses of intercollegiate athletic programs: Financial trends and relationships.* Overland Park, KS: National Collegiate Athletic Association.

Fulks, D. L. (1995). *Revenues and expenses of intercollegiate athletic programs: Financial trends and relationships.* Overland Park, KS: National Collegiate Athletic Association.

Fulks, D. L. (1997). *Revenues and expenses of intercollegiate athletic programs: Financial trends and relationships.* Overland Park, KS: National Collegiate Athletic Association.

Harris, Louis. (1991). *The public and the media's understanding and assessment of the NCAA.* New York: National Collegiate Athletic Association.

National Association of Athletics Compliance Coordinators. (1995, Summer). Final television survey results in. *NAACC Quarterly, 9,* 1.

National Association of College and University Business Officers. (1993). *The financial management of intercollegiate athletics programs.* Washington, DC: NACUBO Athletic Programs Advisory Committee.

Rudolph, F. (1990). *The American college and university: A history.* Athens: University of Georgia Press.

Thelin, J. R. & Wiseman, L. L. (1989). *The old college try: Balancing athletics and academics in higher education* (Report No. 4). Washington, DC: George Washington University.

Torpor, B. (1995, March). Athletics and marketing. *Marketing higher education, IX*(3), 6.

Wolff, A. (1995, June). Broken beyond repair. *Sports Illustrated, 82*(23), 20–26.

PART II

The Preparation of Coaches and Administrators

C OACHES AND ATHLETIC ADMINISTRATORS justify their involvement with young people on the basis that they are educators. The playing field or court, they say, is their classroom and the lessons taught there in discipline, teamwork, and sportsmanship are just as important as the lessons taught in the lecture hall, chemistry lab, or at home. Ironically, there are virtually no educational standards or criteria for becoming a coach; all one needs is a whistle. In the case of athletic administrators, while training programs exist in the form of bachelor's and master's degrees in sports administration, the focus of those programs is on the business, marketing, and operational, rather than the educational, issues and expectations relating to the job.

From the pee-wee to the major college level, the attitudes and behavior of coaches have a very direct impact on the personal, educational, and athletic development of the athlete. In the case of athletic administrators, while their impact may not be as direct, it is, nonetheless, profound, as they have tremendous influence over the goals and tone of the athletic programs they supervise. As the two authors in this part articulate, given such influence, the issue of the preparation and continued professional development of those who coach and administer athletic programs is absolutely critical.

As Bob Bigelow argued in Chapter 1, the environment within which sports activities occur has a tremendous impact on the athletic, personal, and educational development of youth. It is at the youth sports level that the future high school or college athlete is first introduced to organized sport and that direct parental involvement is greatest. The attitudes and expectations regarding organized athletics instilled in the 10-year-old are carried throughout a lifetime. As Bigelow so aptly pointed out, it is the attitudes and actions of the adults and parents that most directly determine the quality of a child's sports experience.

Michael Clark, of Michigan State University's Institute for the Study of Youth Sport, agrees with Bigelow. In Chapter 5, he calls attention to what may be the single most important factor in conducting youth sports programs that are beneficial and, most important, fun for children—the preparation and education of coaches. According to Clark, the majority of America's youth coaches are people with no formal preparation in fitness training, child development, or first aid; their only coaching credentials are that they are parents, like children, or have an interest in a particular sport. Citing the significant negative implications of placing unprepared coaches in such positions of influence, Clark calls for the adoption and implementation of education programs using nationally agreed-upon standards of coaching competencies.

Clark goes on to argue that such programs also must be developed for college coaches, as they too justify their position on campus on the basis of their being educators. Specifically, Clark calls for an increased emphasis on the academic preparation of coaches as well as the implementation of professional development programs that incorporate components that relate directly to the educational mission of the institution and the academic and personal development of the student-athlete.

The issue of the education, preparation, and professional development does not, however, apply solely to coaches, writes Andrew Kreutzer, coordinator of Ohio University's Sports Administration Program. While knowledge of the management and fiscal intricacies of running an athletic department are important, he writes in Chapter 6, athletic administrators' preparation also must foster an appreciation and understanding of the role of athletics within an educational setting. The institutions most responsible for such preparation, he argues, are colleges and universities that offer degrees in athletic administration. Kreutzer questions the current content of sports administration curricula, calling for an increased emphasis on curricular elements that provide students with a better understanding of the relationship of athletic programs to the educational process as well as the goals and mission of the educational institutions of which they are a part. Such a shift of focus in the preparation of future athletic administrators will serve educational institutions well as they search for ways to more fully integrate athletic programs into the educational community.

Both authors are correct in asserting that with such a strong influence over the lives of young athletes and the programs in which they participate, and such a tremendous potential impact on the goals and mission of the educational institutions of which they are a part, the preparation and professional development of coaches and athletic administrators are of utmost importance.

5

Who's Coaching the Coaches?

Michael A. Clark

Numerous sponsoring groups and agencies provide American youth with a wide variety of opportunities to participate in sports. These range from highly structured, competitive national programs such as Little League baseball to local recreational programs that allow anyone to play. Service clubs, educational institutions, for-profit providers, charitable organizations, and "mom & pop" groups all sponsor programs. However, because no single social or political entity oversees youth sports, solid data about who plays and coaches are difficult to obtain.

Based on various research, it is reasonable to conclude that one-half to two-thirds of American youth play organized sports each year (Ewing & Seefeldt, 1991; Ewing, Seefeldt, & Brown, 1997; Howard, 1992; National Sporting Goods Association, 1995). This would put the number of athletes in the range of 24 to 33 million.

Determining the number of coaches involved in youth sports is more difficult, as they have been counted only in the study by Ewing, Seefeldt, and Brown (1997). There it is reported that 3.1 million coaches were working in all levels of youth sports. Such levels of involvement make our nation a world leader in sports participation. But one critical area in which the United States lags far behind other countries is in the formal preparation of coaches.

Many other nations have well-developed programs for educating coaches. Statements describing what is important for coaches to know at each level of play are common. Many countries require formal training, examinations, certificates, and even licenses to coach. Running counter to this increase in the professionalization of coaches internationally, American sports at all levels remain dominated by truly amateur coaches.

This is especially true of youth sports, where the majority of coaches are people whose only credentials are being parents, liking children, or

145254

having an interest in a sport. How most people go about the actual business of coaching is often based on their observations of how others perform the role. Professional or collegiate coaches on television and memories from their own youth become guides for behavior. At best, the aspiring coach is ill-prepared for the challenges to be met but finds a way to muddle through without doing too much damage. At worst, the person makes poor decisions or acts inappropriately. As a result, athletes and coaches drop out, game officials are needlessly abused, sponsors are frustrated in their efforts to run quality programs, and parents are forced to look elsewhere for their children's recreation and instruction.

THE IMPORTANCE OF COACHES' EDUCATION

In many other countries, coaches are required to undergo extensive preparation to progress through, or even enter, the profession. For example, Canada has a mandatory, national five-level program that has been in place long enough to undergo evaluation and change (Canadian National Certification Program, 1989; National Coaching Certification Council, 1978). Currently the Coaching Association of Canada (1997a, 1997b) is exploring alternative delivery systems while making programs more uniform. In Australia, responsibility for required educational efforts has devolved from the national to the state level. This has caused those sponsoring training programs to rethink their offerings and to find new funding, but groups such as the Coaching Foundation of Western Australia remain committed to providing the required education to all coaches (Edmunds, 1997). In Ireland, a 1985 report found a minority of qualified coaches and the need for a standardized course of preparation. The Irish response included creating a National Coaching and Training Centre and a National Coaching Development Program (Tindall, 1997). As these diverse examples demonstrate, most nations that are competitive in world athletics have programs to educate coaches, including those at the very beginning levels of youth competition. Precise descriptions of content, classes, examinations, and even licensing are common (Campbell, 1993).

Most American coaches, however, have little or no formal preparation for their positions. Nearly 80% of coaches in the 1997 study by Ewing, Seefeldt, and Brown were involved in agency-sponsored and recreational sports, which depend almost exclusively on volunteers. Some sponsoring agencies, such as the American Youth Soccer Organization (AYSO) and USA Hockey, provide certification classes for their member coaches. Often these programs are mandatory only for coaches at certain levels of competition or in specific areas. Consequently, they do not reach all coaches. Sponsors such as Little League, YMCA, and Boys/Girls Clubs also offer educational opportunities to coaches, but seldom are these required. In short, most volunteer youth coaches have few qualifications for holding such critical positions (American Academy of Pediatrics Committee on Physical Fitness, Recreation, and Sports, 1981; Bronzon, 1982).

The remaining 20% of coaches, those in scholastic or club sports and those working in for-profit settings, generally are paid, but even they often lack formal preparation. A survey of requirements found everything from a rigorous, 30-hour program for public school coaches in New York State, to first aid and safety training in Ohio, to Michigan's simply requiring nonfaculty scholastic coaches to be "at least eighteen (18) years of age and not a current high school student" (Michigan High School Athletic Association, 1997, p. 5). Only six states reported mandatory certification requirements of any kind and an additional nine had voluntary programs (Sisley & Wiese, 1987). Often the motivation for coaches' education programs is the growing employment of nonteachers as coaches in educational institutions (Figone, 1994; Frost, 1995; Knorr, 1996).

Volunteer and walk-on coaches may have the best intentions and may even possess a great deal of sport-specific knowledge. Lacking formal training, they coach based on observations of others in the role or by recalling their own experiences as athletes. Professional or collegiate coaches are not necessarily good role models for youth and scholastic coaches. Further, most observation of these coaches is limited to game-day situations. The organizational and teaching skills so necessary for success remain beyond the view of untrained coaches. And modeling the behavior of a former coach does not necessarily serve today's coaches well, as the philosophies and actions so learned may not reflect contemporary theory and practice or the needs of today's youth. In the worst cases, the actions of unprepared coaches may jeopardize the safety of their athletes and constitute a liability exposure for themselves and the program that employs them (Knorr, 1996; Mills & Dunlevy, 1997).

Most coaches, even unprepared volunteers, find ways to help athletes learn, and few become involved in legal proceedings. However, as they muddle through, uneducated coaches may make poor decisions, behave inappropriately, and have unrealistic expectations that may negatively affect their athletes.

WHY KIDS PLAY SPORTS

Good coaches are good teachers. What they do relates directly to why young people enter sports and why they drop out. Coaches who do not

Table 5.1. Reasons for Participating in Sports Given by Youth 10–17 Years
            of Age

Males	Females
1. To improve my skills*	1. To have fun*
2. For the excitement of competition	2. To stay in shape*
3. To do something I'm good at	3. To get exercise*
4. To have fun*	4. To improve my skills*
5. To stay in shape*	5. To do something I'm good at
6. To play as part of a team*	6. To play as part of a team*
7. To win	7. For the excitement of competition
8. To go to a higher level of competition	8. To learn new skills*
9. To get exercise*	9. For the team spirit
10. For the challenge of competition	10. For the challenge of competition

Source: Ewing, M. E., & Seefeldt, V. (1991). p. 41.

understand why children and youth become involved in sports, and why they later may drop out, are unlikely to be able to create a positive participation environment for their athletes.

In 1991, Ewing and Seefeldt reported the reasons for being active in sports cited by nearly 25,000 young people in a national sample. Of the ten leading reasons for participation, five, in the case of males, and six, in the case of females, relate to things a coach affects directly (starred items in Table 5.1). This is especially true for young women; the four top reasons for participation relate to items controlled by coaches. The reasons young people listed for leaving sports reinforce this conclusion. For both genders, six of ten reasons relate directly to things within the control of coaches (Table 5.2). In a 1981 preliminary study, Weinberg reported comparable reasons for participating, and a study of players who had dropped out of ice hockey produced nearly identical results (Walter, Ewing, & Seefeldt, 1995). This research proves that while the athlete, parents, and other concerned adults, as well as social pressures, influence how youth perceive their involvement in sports, it is the attitude, experience, and teaching ability of the coach that have the most dramatic impact on those perceptions (see Tables 5.1 and 5.2).

There is no reason why the United States should lag so far behind in this critical aspect of athletics. *National Standards for Athletic Coaches* have been developed (National Association for Sport and Physical Education, 1995) that outline what coaches should know and be able to do—

Table 5.2. Reasons for Dropping Out of Sports Given by Youth 10–17
    Years of Age

Males	Females
1. No longer interested	1. No longer interested
2. Not having fun *	2. Not having fun*
3. Tired of playing and practicing	3. Too much pressure on me*
4. Sport required too much time*	4. Need more time for school work
5. Sport conflicted with other sports	5. Coach was a poor teacher*
6. Practices and games were boring*	6. Tired of playing and practicing
7. Wanted to participate in non-sports activities	7. Sport required too much time*
8. Coach was a poor teacher*	8. Wanted to participate in non-sport activities
9. Coach played only favorite players*	9. Coach played only favorite players*
10. Too much emphasis on winning*	10. Never felt like I belonged with the team*

Source: Ewing, M. E., & Seefeldt, V. (1991). p. 66.

from practice planning and motivating athletes to providing first aid and making strategic decisions. The *Standards,* spread across five levels of coaching, are incremental and cumulative. At each level, they describe the preparation and experience a coach needs to meet the challenge of working in that competitive situation. Together, they provide an outline for the professionalization of coaching in America.

The first three levels of the *Standards* most directly affect youth play. Level 1 focuses on the people who volunteer their time as coaches and direct an athlete's first sports experiences. Level 5 considers the needs of coaches working at national and international levels of competition.

With the *Standards* established and endorsed by an increasing number of sports organizations, the challenge now is to create formal educational programs that provide coaches a solid knowledge base to enable them to effectively perform their coaching responsibilities. In short, if we want our youth to have quality athletic experiences, the preparation and training of their coaches is absolutely critical.

DEVELOPING STANDARDS

Nearly 50 years ago, a commission created by the National Education Association recommended the certification of scholastic coaches. From 1962 to 1973, the American Association for Health, Physical Education, and Recreation and various other concerned groups jointly sponsored three conferences on coaching, one resulting in proposed minimum expectations for coaches. By the mid-1980s, the National Association for Girls and Women in Sports and the National Association for Sport and Physical Education (NASPE) revisited the issue. A survey of requirements was conducted by Sisley and Wiese (1987), a position paper was produced, and a call was made for educational programs specifically designed to produce skilled coaches. But nearly 4 decades of effort resulted in little more than a broad outline of what coaches needed to know and the general feeling that few of them possessed such knowledge (Knorr, 1996).

More recently, various interests created three competing educational programs aimed at coaches of recreational and scholastic sports: the National Youth Sports Coaches Association, the Program for Athletic Coaches Education, and the American Sports Education Program (Mills & Dunlevy, 1997). The United States Olympic Committee required its constituent national governing bodies to produce educational materials for their coaches (Crawford, 1993). An increasing number of colleges and universities began offering programs intended to prepare coaches, primarily for secondary schools. And national program sponsors such as the YMCA, AYSO, USA Hockey, and Special Olympics created educational materials to be used in preparing coaches.

Unfortunately, attempts to define a set of competencies either emphasized broad elements that begged for specific interpretation or focused tightly on the particular demands of a specific sport. There was no consensus on the essential knowledge and skills for all coaches or on how coaching careers might progress. Much discussion, some turf protecting, and confusion resulted. Nevertheless, various interested parties continued to work toward a generally acceptable statement of what coaches need to know and be able to do. Within the framework of an NASPE task force, these individuals and groups came together several times to assess, discuss, criticize, and reframe proposed coaching competencies. Those with a stake in athletic coaching who did not participate actively in the task force were sought out and given the opportunity to comment on proposed content and language. Once a consensus position was developed, affected parties were given the opportunity to review and endorse the proposal. The end result was a document titled *Quality Coaches, Quality Sports: National Standards for Athletic Coaches (NASPE, 1995).*

THE NATIONAL STANDARDS FOR COACHES

The *Standards* derive from eight broad areas of sport science. Within these domains, the task force presents 37 general statements of essential knowledge, concluding that they "reflect the fundamental competencies that administrators, athletes and the public should expect of athletic coaches at various levels of experience" (NASPE, 1995, p. 2). These statements "cover everything from practice planning to motivating athletes to providing first aid and making strategic decisions." Each standard is supported by a number of more specific descriptions of the knowledge required of coaches. Referred to as "competencies," these are tied to various levels of coaching. A competency may be described as necessary for beginning coaches (Level 1) or as more appropriate to the needs of entry-level scholastic coaches or those working with highly skilled athletes (Level 3). Similarly, competencies may be described as requiring "Awareness, Application or Mastery" by coaches at a particular level (NASPE, 1995, pp. 4–5).

For example, in the "Injuries: Prevention, Care and Management" domain (prevent injuries by recognizing and insisting on safe playing conditions), the beginning (Level 1) coach must master how to "establish and follow procedures for identifying and correcting unsafe conditions" and be prepared to "stop or modify practices or play when unsafe conditions exist." To "know that safety equipment, coach's vigilance, and other safe-guards provide protection against injury to athletes," is expected to be part of a coach's awareness at Level 2 and to be mastered at Level 3 (NASPE, 1995, p. 15). There are nearly 320 incremental competencies that outline the essential knowledge and skills for coaches. The collection of competencies to be mastered at each level of coaching, combined with on-the-job experience, provides the knowledge required for progression to the next level.

The *Standards* are neither a certification program nor an assessment program. Rather, they are a consensus description of the essential knowledge and experience required of coaches at various levels of competition. The *Standards* are not sport-specific. Instead, they provide a framework for creating educational programs that meet the needs of prospective and inservice coaches. Organizations responsible for certifying, educating, evaluating, or developing coaches should not view themselves as being constrained by the *Standards;* instead, they should see their efforts as being empowered. With the *Standards* in place, sponsoring groups can concentrate on interpreting them within the context of appropriate sport- and situation-specific programs. This is especially important to agencies involved in youth sports, as Levels 1 through 3 directly relate to them. Finally, the *Standards* are not the last word on what coaches need to know and to be able to do. Rather, members of the task force responsible for them acknowledge that "new information will demand that the standards be reviewed and updated on a regular basis" (NASPE, 1995, p. 2). In the meantime, advocates of the *Standards* are working together to evaluate existing educational programs, to encourage new ones, and to influence the direction of future efforts.

IMPROVING THE ATHLETIC EXPERIENCE

Critics of the movement toward standards fear a reduction in the number of likely coaching candidates if the time or financial demands of educational programs become too great. Some fear a loss of local institutional control. Others are philosophically opposed to any sort of "national" effort or are concerned that educating coaches will increase sponsors' liability exposure (Smith, 1983). While these doubts represent problems to be addressed, it is, however, more important to consider the benefits of formal training programs, particularly for youth coaches.

Research suggests that there is a complex, but important, relationship among the coach's believed ability to affect learning and performance of athletes, the satisfaction of the athletes, and measures of coaching success (Feltz, Chase, Moritz, & Sullivan, 1997). Further, it has been found that coaches taking part in formal educational programs become more convinced of their ability to positively influence their athletes and events (Malete, 1997).

This work derives, in part, from efforts to understand what makes educators effective. Studies of teachers' efficacy have found that those with a heightened sense of their capability have longer careers and are more committed to the profession (Coladarci, 1992). Although not entirely replicated in the field of coaching, this line of research implies something crucial to the long-term success of programs: Coaches who have confidence in their own ability to influence the learning and performance of their athletes will in fact be more effective coaches and likely will remain active much longer. Additionally, these people probably will promote athletics and coaching as positive experiences for those involved and may become effective recruiters of new coaches. As is suggested in Malete's (1997) work, participation in a formal education program significantly influences how coaches perceive their abilities. Consequently, it might be that education programs actually would aid in attracting and retaining coaches.

Finally, since they are designed to "ensure the enjoyment, safety and positive skill development of America's athletes" (NASPE, 1995, p. 2), the *Standards* should influence coaches to be more concerned with the well-being of the total athlete. This will result in a more positive and beneficial experience for athletes at all levels of sport.

While the focus of this chapter has been on the importance of providing training programs for youth and scholastic coaches, the same issues and concerns apply to coaches at the college level. While college coaches continue to claim they are teachers and educators, it is ironic that virtually no educational standards or criteria exist for becoming a college coach. How can we expect coaches to be positive educational role models when they often have not invested in the educational process themselves? And once hired, they must have the opportunity to refine their teaching skills and develop more fully as educators.

> Professional development opportunities must be broadened to incorporate components that relate more closely to the general purposes of the institution, of higher education, and the educational development of the student-athlete. . . . Presenting issues in student development will raise awareness of the many challenges facing today's college students. Helping coaches use effective retention strategies will facilitate the student-athlete's adjustment to college, thus reducing the likelihood of transfer or withdrawal. Coaches must be encouraged to consider the educational responsibilities inherent in being a member of an academic community. They must understand that their jobs entail more than simply game strategies and training techniques. (Gerdy, 1997, p. 103)

WHO IS COACHING THE COACHES?

Youth and scholastic coaches hold positions of tremendous influence in the lives of the over 30 million young people who play sports annually. Yet, despite the fact that research clearly indicates that formal education programs positively influence a coach's ability to affect learning and performance as well as the satisfaction of athletes with the competitive experience, such programs seldom are mandatory and reach only a small minority of the nation's approximately 3 million youth coaches. By all indications, most of America's coaches are learning about the job from other coaches, whether professional, collegiate, or those for whom they played.

If we are to improve the coaching profession and further enhance the playing experience of young athletes, the issue of how we "coach the coaches" is critical and must assume a more important place in our dialogue regarding sport in America. By outlining a number of relevant competencies in the National Standards for Athletic Coaches, the National Association for Sport and Physical Education has created a framework for discussion and action. By incorporating "Quality Coaches, Quality Sports" in the document's formal title, NASPE has clearly defined the challenge: The quality of coaching determines the quality of the sports experience. Only by providing coaches with formal education, drawing on the cumulative knowledge of sport science, can we provide our youth a positive sports experience.

REFERENCES

American Academy of Pediatrics Committee on Physical Fitness, Recreation, and Sports. (1981). A national program for developing competency in youth sports coaching. Evanston, IL: Author.

Bronzon, R. T. (1982). Preparing leaders for non-school youth sports. *Athletic Training and Facilities, 6,* 12–16.

Campbell, S. (1993). Coaching education around the world. *Sport Science Review,* 2(2), 62–74.

Canadian National Certification Program. (1989). The course conductor: Levels 1–5, theory. Gloucester, Ontario: Coaching Association of Canada.

Coaching Association of Canada. (1997a, December 12). Levels 1–3 [Online]. (Available at http://www.coach.ca/profdev/level13.html)

Coaching Association of Canada. (1997b, December 12). Program delivery options [Online]. (Available at http://www.coach.ca/profdev/progdel.html)

Coladarci, T. (1992). Teachers' sense of efficacy and commitment to teaching. *Journal of Applied Sport Psychology, 60*(4), 323–337.

Crawford, T. (1993). Where are we headed? *Olympic Coach, 3*(4), 1.

Edmunds, J. (1997). Chairperson's report. *Coaching Connection, 4*(3), 2.

Ewing, M. E., & Seefeldt, V. (1991). *Participation and attrition patterns in American agency-sponsored and interscholastic sports.* East Lansing: Michigan State University, Institute for the Study of Youth Sports.

Ewing, M. E., Seefeldt, V., & Brown, T. (1997). *The role of organized sport in the education of children and youth.* New York: Carnegie Corporation.

Feltz, D. L., Chase, M. A., Moritz, S. E., & Sullivan, P. J. (1997). *The development and validation of the coaching efficacy scale.* Unpublished manuscript, Michigan State University, East Lansing.

Figone, A. J. (1994). Origins of the teacher-coach role: Idealism, convenience and unworkability. *The Physical Educator, 51*(1), 148–156.

Frost, J. (1995). A good coach is hard to find. *Executive Educator, 17*(8), 25–27.

Gerdy, J. R. (1997). *The successful college athletic program: The new standard.* Phoenix, AZ: American Council on Education/Oryx Press.

Howard, D. R. (1992). Participation rates in selected sport and fitness activities. *Journal of Sport Management, 6*(3), 191–205.

Knorr, J. (1996). The need to rethink coaching certification. *Scholastic Coach and Athletic Director, 65*(6), 4, 6–7.

Malete, L. (1997). *The effect of a program for athletic coaches education on coaching efficacy.* Unpublished master's thesis, Michigan State University, East Lansing.

Michigan High School Athletic Association. (1997). *Coaches guidebook.* East Lansing: Author.

Mills, B. D., & Dunlevy, S. M. (1997). Coaching certification: What's out there and what needs to be done? *International Journal of Physical Education, 34*(1), 17–26.

National Association for Sport and Physical Education (NASPE). (1995). *Quality coaches, quality sports: National standards for athletic coaches.* Reston, VA: Author.

National Coaching Certification Council. (1978). *National coaching certification program.* Ottawa, Ontario: Author.

National Sporting Goods Association. (1995). *Sports participation in 1994.* Mt. Prospect, IL: Author.

Sisley, B. L., & Wiese, D. M. (1987). Current status: Requirements for interscholastic coaches. Results of NAGWS/NASPE coaching certification survey. *Journal of Physical Education, Recreation and Dance, 58*(7), 73–85.

Smith, R. (1983). Keeping the quality in coaching or the quantity of coaches? *Sports Coach, 7*(1), 2–5.

Tindall, R. (1997). On the road. *Coaching Connection, 4*(3), 6.

Walter, S. A., Ewing, M. E., Seefeldt, V. (1995). *Participation patterns of former youth ice hockey players.* East Lansing: Michigan State University, Institute for the Study of Youth Sports.

6

The Education of Sports Administrators

Andrew Kreutzer

Forty years ago, Walter O'Malley, then owner of the Los Angeles Dodgers, wrote a letter to James G. Mason, a faculty member at the University of Miami, posing the question:

> Where would one go to find a person who by virtue of education had been trained to administer a marina, race track, ski resort, auditorium, stadium, theatre, convention or exhibition hall, or a person to fill an executive position at a team or league level in junior athletics such as Little League baseball, football, scouting, CYO, and youth activities, etc. . . . A course that would enable a graduate to read architectural and engineering plans; or having to do with specifications and contract letting, the functions of a purchasing agent in plant operations. There would be problems of ticket selling and accounting, concessions, sale of advertising in programs, and publications, outdoor and indoor displays and related items. . . .

It was from this letter that Mason first outlined a curriculum to prepare students to meet the vast array of responsibilities O'Malley described. Although the program was not implemented at Coral Gables, it became the basis for the country's first master's program in sports administration.

On leaving Miami, Mason joined the physical education faculty at Ohio University and brought his idea for a sports administration graduate program with him. In 1966, he officially proposed the new course of study. The curriculum was adopted and the first students were admitted. The early curriculum was an adaptation of a traditional physical education program. Through the end of the 1960s, the program developed and each year the number of interested students increased. At the same time, specific courses related to sports administration were developed. Today, the Ohio program continues to flourish, as do similar programs across the country. Sports administration, or sports management, proved to be an idea whose time had arrived. It has been one of the fastest-growing disciplines both on a national and international level.

According to Thomas Sawyer (1993), physical education professor at Indiana State University, the traditional focus of physical education departments had been to prepare teachers and coaches for public schools. But the 1970s brought a time of social change that established the groundwork for a shift in this focus, resulting in the growth and development of the sports administration field. Physical education departments began to see their enrollment decline in the 1970s. A change in the composition of the interscholastic coaching ranks, a decline in the demand for physical educators and resultant enrollment decline in physical education programs, and growth in the number of girls' sports offered, caused physical education departments to expand their curricula to include more non-teaching alternatives.

The 1970s also witnessed industry changes, with the growth of professional soccer, and fitness and recreation clubs and the passing of the American Basketball Association and World Team Tennis. In addition, the rise of double-digit inflation affected all businesses, including sports organizations (Sawyer, 1993). Such change further highlighted the sports industry's need for business-oriented, as well as sports-minded, individuals to lead them. By 1978, there were 20 graduate programs in sports management/sports administration nationwide.

By 1985, the number of programs offered at both the graduate and undergraduate levels had reached 86. Not only were sports administration programs being created, but trade journals and organizations related to the growing field were being developed. The North American Society for Sport Management (NASSM) was founded in 1985, and in 1986 the National Association for Sport and Physical Education (NASPE) formed a task force to study sports management. Both groups promoted research, scholarship, and professional preparation.

Journals such as ARENA, The Journal of Park and Recreation Administration, and SPORTS entered the marketplace in the 1980s. Articles highlighted the need for research specific to the field of sports management, focused on defining the discipline, and identified the most appropriate curricula for undergraduate and graduate programs. The development of trade journals introduced another tool into the industry, whose potential has yet to be fully explored.

Growth in the field continued into the 1990s and, with it, many questions have been raised about supply and demand, accreditation, and changing expectations. Are there too many programs preparing too many prospects for the job market? On what basis and to what ends are curricula being designed? And what exactly are these programs teaching students about the dynamic world of professional athletics and, in the case of youth, school-based, and college sports, about education? And are these programs improving the caliber of managers in the sports industry? These are the issues that will be discussed in this chapter.

ISSUES OF ACCREDITATION

As might have been expected, the dramatic increase in the number of programs led to questions regarding the market's ability to absorb the growing number of graduates and the applicability and quality of program curricula. Concerns grew into a demand for the development and implementation of curriculum standards. To that end, NASPE and, later, NASSM, through a joint task force, began a process of developing program standards in an effort to promote the quality of sports management education on a national scope. Their efforts produced a set of curriculum standards for undergraduate and graduate sports management degree programs and, using these standards, an accreditation model. While these standards generally are recognized and accepted, the model used to develop them is open to criticism, and their applicability to the broad range of sports organizations needs to be scrutinized.

Inherent in any accreditation system is restricted access to the market. Accepting this premise leads to the question of other benefits of, and even potential motives for, supporting accreditation. Does accreditation serve to provide students and the industry with greater assurance of adequate education and preparation for an extremely competitive labor market? Does accreditation serve to protect students from their own unrealistic expectations, or to protect the industry from a flood of underprepared applicants? Or might it serve to shelter those programs that meet current standards from unwanted, and possibly innovative, competition? Even the best-intentioned and most well-designed models can produce positive answers to the preceding questions.

For example, if 200 graduate and undergraduate programs each sent only 25 graduates into the job market annually, there would be 5,000 new, eager sports managers looking for meaningful employment each year. There are simply not enough management or preprofessional job openings to meet that level of demand. In 1986, Tim Gleason, then Assistant Executive Director of the National Association of College Directors of Athletics, said, "Sports administration is a fabulous concept. It is needed in our profession. Let's not destroy a good thing by overkill" (p. 11). Since Gleason's statement, many additional colleges and universities have added programs in sports management.

In any accreditation effort, a delicate balance must be struck between the identification of specific program and curricular standards to ensure quality control and the need for an appropriate degree of flexibility to adapt to the dynamics of a changing marketplace. These challenges were particularly difficult in the case of sports administration because of the tremendous diversity in the field. For example, the curriculum needed to adequately prepare a high school athletic director is different from that needed for the general manager of a professional sports franchise. While there are common skills needed by both of these administrators, their job responsibilities are vastly different. A "one curriculum fits all" model cannot meet the needs of such a diverse industry.

By insisting on compliance with a specific set of curriculum elements, as suggested by the NASPE/NASSM joint task force, schools and programs are forced into concrete standards, which may become roadblocks to legitimate constructive change. As an alternative to the accreditation model based on strict compliance, "strengths should be weighed against weaknesses to evaluate the total pattern of the program" (North Central Association of Colleges and Schools, 1988, p. 3). A model that measures a program against its mission and objectives can be successful without the requirements noted in the NASPE/NASSM model. For example, how did the task force arrive at 20% as the in-unit credit hour minimum for undergraduate programs? Why not 25% or 15%?

Of further concern in the development of these standards was the noticeable lack of participation by practitioners in the field. While the early NASPE group included a few practitioners, the joint task force did not, and the current committee on accreditation has no one outside of academia. The source of new theory and particularly the practical application of theory often are found outside the academic realm. Those individuals who developed the accreditation standards, while identified for their work in the "field," weren't actually "in the field" but rather were academicians who taught sports management. And while the recommendations of the joint task force were presented at four national (academic) conventions, no one who was actually working as an athletic administrator on a daily basis was part of the group responsible for developing curriculum to prepare students for the challenges of the sports administration workplace.

The potential drawbacks of such an omission are obvious. If NASPE wanted to establish the most meaningful and relevant curricular and program standards, it should have included practitioners who had distinguished themselves in the industry and should have considered their input when attempting to forecast trends within the discipline.

ASSESSING A "NEEDS GAP"

While the work of the joint NASPE/NASSM task force has produced comprehensive recommendations for sports management curriculum, there is still the potential for a significant "needs gap" in the education and preparation of many sports management students. This gap is most evident in the preparation of athletics administrators working within educational institutions. Courses that address the "bottom-line" management philosophies of professional sports and of many athletics facilities are becoming more attractive to students who are preparing for careers within educational settings. Balancing the budget by generating additional revenues has become the principal benchmark of a good sports manager. Negotiating broadcast contracts, increasing sponsorship relations, expanding licensing agreements, and adding suites to the stadium and arena are viewed as the highest achievements. While in professional sports these achievements are often consistent with the vision, mission, and objectives of the organizations, they are now becoming the mantras of the college athletics administrator.

Certainly, an understanding of marketing and fund raising is important to any manager. Understanding how these elements fit into the mission of a college or high school athletics department, however, is of equal or greater importance. Sports management students who stand awestruck at the sight of a multimillion dollar campus athletic facility whose primary purpose is to glamorize the recruiting process for a limited number of blue-chip recruits, find it difficult to answer when asked if there could be another way to allocate those same resources to better serve the mission of the institution. Do sports management students even understand the process through which educational institutions identify their missions? Strategic planning, a process that takes vision and mission and translates them into action, is a critical management function as fundamental to organizational success as marketing or finance.

There is adequate evidence to suggest that, in spite of sports management curricula, major problems continue to plague college athletic programs. Gender equity as a management issue has been "on the books" since 1972. How difficult and complex must a problem be to take over a quarter of a century to solve? Do all NCAA Division I student-athletes actually limit their sports involvement to only 20 hours a week? And what does this sports involvement teach the student-athlete who is asked to sign a false or misleading document regarding those 20 hours? In short, there is more to leading an athletic department that is housed within an educational institution than marketing, promotions, and game management, which are the types of courses the NASPE/NASSM accreditation model emphasizes.

THE OPPORTUNITY TO INFLUENCE

The importance of sports management curriculum content goes beyond simply providing students with a more thorough background to succeed in an increasingly diverse sports marketplace. Specifically, it represents an opportunity for sports management professors, through their programs and the students who graduate from them, to assume a more active and direct role in shaping sport's influence in our culture. The traditional role of sports administration faculty has been to observe, comment, and teach about various aspects of sport. While faculty have had an impact on certain areas of sports management, particularly the areas of marketing, facility management, and personnel management, their influence in the area of educational reform and athletics' role in that reform, has been minimal. While many faculty write and comment, often critically, on the role of high school or college sport, it is through curriculum reform that they can have the greatest and most lasting impact on the future of sport in America.

Take, for example, the ongoing effort to "reform" big-time college athletics, one of higher education's most pressing issues. It is no secret that the fundamental challenge facing higher education leaders is to effectively integrate athletic programs into the academic community to more closely tie athletic department goals, programs, and outcomes to those of the university. The concern is that athletic programs are more about winning, making money, and providing entertainment than about education, and as a result are not contributing to the mission of the university in meaningful ways.

A key causal factor in this conflict is the fact that many coaches and athletic administrators have an inadequate understanding of, appreciation for, and sensitivity to the role, purpose, and priorities of higher education. While we have prepared our sports management students to perform the core business functions necessary to operate an athletic department, it is arguable whether they have been instilled with a strong sense of educational mission, including knowledge of and appreciation for the challenges facing higher education and the athletic department's role in helping to meet those challenges.

For example, an athletic director who appreciates and understands the dynamics of higher education's constant struggle in the area of resource acquisition and allocation will be more sensitive in stewarding athletic department budgets in a way that serves the goals and mission of the university rather than simply the purposes of the athletic department. An athletic director with a clear sense of higher education's teaching function may be more inclined to evaluate coaches on criteria other than strictly wins and losses. And athletic leaders with an understanding of student development and retention concepts will likely be more sensitive to student-athlete welfare concerns. If athletic programs are going to fully realize their potential to contribute to the mission of higher education in lasting and meaningful ways, the athletic administrator of the future must be trained using an educationally centered curriculum, rather than solely the business-centered curriculum suggested by the accreditation model.

Sports management programs are in a position to have a very direct, long-term impact on issues facing not only higher education, but high school education as well as sport at the youth level. Only through the development of a more educationally centered sports management curriculum will future youth, high school, and college athletic administrators obtain the background necessary to provide the leadership that can ensure that our nation's sports programs complement, rather than undermine, educational goals and processes.

ELEMENTS OF AN EDUCATIONALLY CENTERED CURRICULUM

Clearly, sports management programs have done well in preparing students to perform the core business and management functions required of sports administrators. But as mentioned earlier, the "one curriculum fits all" approach to preparing athletic administrators falls short of meeting the needs of a diverse marketplace. Perhaps we would better serve students who plan to pursue a career in youth, high school, or college athletics by preparing them to be not athletic administrators, but rather academic administrators with a concentration in athletics. Using this framework as a point of reference, an educationally centered, but athletically related, curriculum could be designed.

For example, courses in higher education structure and finance, governance, as well as current issues should be required. Courses in student personnel and development would be an important element of such a program, as would a course relating to teaching methodology (after all, coaches and athletic administrators justify their place within an educational institution on the basis that they are teachers and educators). And with violations of NCAA regulations and concerns regarding a general decline in sportsmanship at all levels of play, offerings in ethics would provide a foundation for a better understanding of principles regarding academic and institutional integrity and fair play.

Rather than students fulfilling their practicum, internship, and work-study obligations only in the athletic department, they should be required to work in the office of an academic dean, provost, high school principal, or other academic officer. Such practical academic experience will serve those who wish to pursue a career in high school or college athletics far more effectively than being one of many interns in a ticket office.

In sum, the current model requires that sports marketing and sports governance be included as content areas within an accredited program's curriculum, but does not address courses that might help students negotiate the swirling, political waters of a university or even a high school campus. Will students who aspire to jobs as college athletic directors be required to study the structure of higher education, or the role of higher education in society? Will they be taught how to manage diversity in an educational setting?

Could it be that in its movement from a physical education to a management-based perspective of curriculum, sports management misplaced its sense of educational mission?

In 1987, Stephen Hardy noted that sports management curricula needed to "produce people capable of managing sport organizations to higher levels of quality and productivity" (p. 208). If the ills frequently associated with college, and increasingly high school, athletics are to be rectified, the task will start with good management. And students being prepared to enter the field, our athletic administrators of the future, are greatly influenced by the focus, emphasis, and priorities of their sports management curriculum.

REFERENCES

Gleason, T. (1986, February). Sports administration degrees: growing to fill a need/supply overwhelms demand. *Athletic Administration*, pp. 10–11.

Hardy, S. (1987). Graduate curriculums in sport management: The need for a business orientation. *Quest, 39*, 207–216.

North Central Association of Colleges and Schools. (1988). *A handbook of accreditation*. Chicago: The Commission.

Sawyer, T. (1993). Sport management: Where should it be housed? *Journal of Physical Education, Recreation and Dance, 64*, 4–5.

PART III

Race and Gender in Sport

THE ISSUES OF race and gender equity in sport are so widely discussed and written about that it might appear that combining them in one part of the book is trivializing their significance. They are grouped together here because they are so important that no book on sport would be complete without their discussion. Rather than engaging in a comprehensive discussion of the various intricacies of these issues (Entire books have been written on each subject!), the intent was to focus on the narrower issue of the effect of race and gender as it applies specifically to educational opportunity and expectations.

It is precisely because so much has been written about these issues that there is a tendency to become desensitized to them. The discussion continues, however, due to the highly emotional nature of the issues themselves as well as the belief of many that there has been very little meaningful progress in either area.

These issues continue to generate such hotly contested debate for another reason. One of the primary justifications for our tremendous educational investment in sport is the very powerful notion that athletics opens various doors of opportunity for participants, most notably, the opportunity to realize upward mobility through education. Closely related to this belief is the claim that sport is perhaps the only institution in America in which the playing field is truly level, where all individuals, regardless of race, creed, or ethnicity, are evaluated and rewarded based on identical criteria—athletic performance. Any coach, for example, will tell you that he or she is interested not in the color of an athlete's skin, but only in his or her on-the-field production.

When the issues of race and gender are discussed, it is, however, the same small group of "sports theorists" who are asked to comment—the same people, the same arguments, and the same calls for action. While these perspectives have been, and continue to be, valuable, fresh viewpoints on the topics are needed. To that end, two recently graduated Black student-athletes who played major college football were asked to contribute. Not only have these two writers experienced firsthand, the pressures and demands of playing NCAA Division I-A football and the realities of being a highly visible Black student-athlete on an overwhelmingly White campus—something that most writers on the subject can only observe and imagine—but both have remained involved in the lives of student-athletes as athletic department advisors in the areas of academics and student-athlete welfare. They were, and remain, on the front lines of the battle for educational opportunity and racial equality in athletics. Their experience is current, it is real, it is unique. Their perspective is important and, prior to this, largely unheard.

In Chapter 7, Derrick Gragg, Assistant Athletic Director for Compliance at the University of Michigan, addresses the claim that athletics is a powerful tool to integrate Blacks into the educational community and, later, mainstream society. Gragg argues that because of the common and well-documented acts of exploitation of Black athletes, such claims are suspect at best. He suggests that the perceptions regarding, and treatment of, Black athletes actually serve to alienate, rather than integrate, them from the mainstream academic community and society in general. Nonetheless, Gragg believes that athletics can foster such integration and offers specific suggestions to help our educational institutions realize athletics' potential in this regard.

Darren Bilberry follows with an examination of the claim that athletics provides meaningful educational opportunity for Blacks. Bilberry suggests that such claims are largely untrue, simply another myth perpetuated by the sports establishment to justify its ill-conceived relationship with our country's educational system. The author argues that the supposed educational opportunity afforded through athletics is not an educational opportunity at all, but simply an athletic one. Because it is only through meaningful educational opportunity that genuine integration can occur off the fields of play, he concludes that the widely held claim that athletics offers a genuine chance for upward mobility for Blacks is, in most cases, false. Bilberry goes beyond the common calls for institutional initiatives and reform to address the problem, and challenges Black athletes, coaches, and administrators themselves to take more responsibility for holding the athletic establishment accountable on its promise of genuine educational opportunity through athletics.

Interestingly, both writers cite White coaches', teachers', and athletic administrators' tendency to stereotype Black athletes, expecting far less of them academically and socially as compared with their White teammates, as a major cause of Black athlete exploitation. As has been well documented, educational performance is largely affected by the level of expectations of teachers, parents, coaches, and other adults. That these authors, both products of the current athletic system, would identify the lack of high academic and social expectations of Blacks as an issue of great importance, is significant and warrants continued research, discussion, and attention.

Turning to the issue of gender, Darlene Bailey, Associate Athletic Director at Southwest Missouri State University, offers a unique perspective on opportunity, or lack thereof, for women in athletics. The writer argues that the most critical issue on the gender equity front is not participation opportunities, scholarship dollars, or coaches' salaries, but the continued lack of women in administrative leadership positions. Based on research findings on the positive impact of the growing number of women in leadership positions in the corporate world, she suggests that women are uniquely qualified to help address many of the issues currently facing the athletic community. Bailey maintains that the importance of providing more women the opportunity to work with men to shape the future of both men's and women's athletic programs goes far beyond the issue of equality, representing perhaps the final chance for high school and college athletics to be structured and conducted in a way that contributes in very direct and meaningful ways to the educational goals of our schools and colleges.

7

Race in Athletics: Integration or Isolation?

Derrick Gragg

In 1916, Brown University's Frank Pollard became the first nationally known Black football star at a predominantly White institution. While Pollard opened the door, it was not until after World War II, which brought a huge influx of Black students to campuses under the G. I. Bill, that the list of black football stars became staggering (Orr, 1969). But despite the fact that Black student-athletes now constitute the majority of participants in the high-visibility, revenue-generating sports of football and basketball, the story regarding the integration of both high school and college sports remains a sad one. In spite of proving their worth on the fields and courts, Black student-athletes, as well as Black coaches and administrators, remain second-class citizens, isolated and discriminated against by the very institution they played so vital a role in building.

Notwithstanding the harsh realities facing Blacks in sports, athletics continues to be portrayed as our educational system's best tool to promote racial integration and tolerance. Coaches, for example, trumpet the virtues of sport as an integrationist tool, proclaiming to be "color blind" when evaluating athletic performance. Sports proponents argue that athletics encourages people of different nationalities, cultures, and ethnicities to work together in the pursuit of a common goal. In large part, athletics is justified within our educational system as the only activity that offers a true intersection of race, gender, and ethnicity. While this may be true in theory, reality suggests that stereotypes, exploitation, and racism are alive and well in athletics, resulting not in the integration of Blacks into educational or mainstream society, but in their further separation and isolation.

EXPLOITATION OF THE BLACK STUDENT-ATHLETE

Although a large number of college programs have been built on their
talents, these same programs show little concern for the long-term personal and academic welfare of Black student-athletes. Perhaps the most
visible example of exploitation is that of Dexter Manley. Manley, a former
all-pro football player for the Super Bowl champion Washington Red-
skins, announced years ago to a U.S. Senate panel that he attended Oklahoma State University for 4 years despite the fact that he could not read.
Memphis State University (now the University of Memphis), a participant
in the 1985 NCAA Final Four, went 12 years without graduating a single
Black basketball player (Lapchick, 1991). Apparently, these are not isolated incidences. According to the NCAA, only 37% of minority student-
athletes in the entering classes of 1983–84 through 1986–87 graduated
within 6 years of initial enrollment (NCAA, 1996a, 1996b).

Thus, it is no surprise that many Black student-athletes feel they are
used and simply discarded after their playing days are over. This feeling
of isolation and disenfranchisement is particularly acute as these student-
athletes feel they are bankrolling sports programs played mainly by
Whites. The predominantly Black football and men's basketball teams
generate 91% of yearly NCAA revenue (Fish, 1997b); revenue that is used
to finance other programs such as tennis, golf, and swimming.

Less obvious than poor graduation rates is the fact that Black
student-athletes are usually at the center of most major college sports
scandals, raising interesting questions regarding exploitation. Although
the NCAA does not chart the racial makeup of student-athletes involved
in violations, former director of enforcement David Berst acknowledges
that "a large proportion of those are black." (Fish, 1997a). Former NCAA
investigator Mike Glazier, an attorney who represents colleges in NCAA
infractions cases, puts the figure at 90% for football and men's basketball
(Fish, 1997b).

Does this mean that coaches and athletic administrators expect less
from Black athletes on issues relating to ethics, or simply that many Black
student-athletes come from economically disadvantaged backgrounds
and thus are more likely to accept such inducements? Could it mean that
the predominantly White athletic establishment considers the relationship between Black student-athletes and their institutions a business,
rather than an educational, association? Are coaches more inclined to provide Black student-athletes with money and perks, thus reinforcing the
myth that the key to future financial and personal success is through
athletics, rather than education?

While student-athletes must be held accountable for their actions, it is also true that young people behave according to what is expected of them by people of influence in their lives. Obviously, coaches have a great amount of influence over student-athletes. The fact that these very influential adults, who cast themselves as "teachers," are initiating actions that are clearly against the rules, sends a very powerful message to student-athletes—that it is winning, rather than education and ethical responsibility, that is important.

But the exploitation of Black student-athletes is not confined to our college and university athletic departments. Derek Sparks, a former running back for Washington State University, is an example of how Black student-athletes are being exploited at the high school level. Between grades 9 and 12, Sparks attended four different high schools. While attempting to transfer from Montclair Prep to Mater Dei high school in California, his transcript apparently was altered by Montclair Prep officials intent on preventing him from having the necessary grade point average to transfer. Sparks later brought suit against Montclair Prep and won a favorable settlement against the high school. He also alleged that a member of the Montclair Prep staff offered a car and money if he transferred to Montclair from Banning High school in the spring of 1988. A school official also was mentioned as offering Sparks a Porsche if he attended the University of Southern California upon graduation (Spencer, 1994).

While Sparks's case may represent the extreme, the exploitation of Black student-athletes at the high school level is not uncommon. The most prevalent form of abuse involves the "passing along" of student-athletes from grade to grade, regardless of whether they are qualified to pass. Thus, even at the high school level, the long-term educational best interests of the Black student-athlete is sacrificed for short-term athletic gain.

FIGHTING STEREOTYPES

A common misperception is that Black athletes, due to their "star status," are readily embraced by the campus and surrounding communities. Other than during game time, however, quite the opposite is the case. From the moment they set foot on campus, Black student-athletes face a constant struggle to overcome stereotypes and negative labels. Many faculty members, for example, resent the presence of Black student-athletes on campus, feeling they are underqualified students who attend universities at the expense of better qualified White students.

Not only must Black student-athletes overcome the stereotype of the "unprepared Black student," but they also must fight the "dumb jock" label. The resulting combination of these powerful stereotypes makes it very difficult to be taken seriously as a student, because many peers, faculty members, and administrators view the "dumb, Black, unprepared athlete" as being on campus only to score touchdowns, make jump shots, or set track and field records. While White student-athletes face similar stereotypes, they can integrate more easily into the general campus community because of the color of their skin. It is, however, very difficult for a Black student-athlete to "disappear" in a classroom or campus at a predominantly White institution.

Coaches, faculty, and administrators are not the only ones who perpetuate such stereotypes. The media magnifies such negativity as well. For example, from 1988 through 1990, there were 30 newspaper accounts of athletes who were charged with some form of sexual assault against women. Twenty-one of the 30 were White athletes, yet the only cover story done by *Sports Illustrated* on this issue was about Black athletes charged with these offenses while playing at Oklahoma and Colorado (Lapchick, 1991).

While the purpose of this chapter is not to dwell on these well-documented transgressions, they must be mentioned because they have a very direct effect on the issue of the integration of the Black student-athlete into the mainstream high school or college community and, later, into mainstream society. These acts of exploitation, whether academic, ethical, or having to do with lower expectations or the perpetuation of racial stereotypes, all seem to occur more often to Black student-athletes than to White. These perceptions and abuses serve not to integrate, but to further isolate, the Black student-athlete, not only from the general student body, but other from student-athletes as well. Thus, the claim that athletics is an effective way in which to promote the integration of Blacks into the educational or societal mainstream is suspect at best.

DISENFRANCHISED COACHES AND ADMINISTRATORS

Black coaches and administrators are similarly disenfranchised from the athletic establishment. While accepted as being able to perform well enough as players to lead teams on the field, they have yet to be embraced as leaders who have the skills and intelligence to coach or oversee programs. Although African-Americans constitute 63% of all Division I men's basketball players and 53% of all football players (Fish, 1997b), Black coaches are greatly underrepresented in both sports. According to a 1995 NCAA report, only 3% of the head football coaches at predominantly White institutions (three of 107 schools) were Black (Blauvelt & Carey, 1995). Black assistant coaches made up less than 10% of all Division I football staffs (Lapchick, 1996). Throughout the 100-plus-year history of college football, only 14 African-American men served as head football coaches at predominantly White institutions. The Southeastern Conference, which may have more Black football players than any other conference, has yet to hire a Black head football coach. In nonrevenue-generating sports such as track and field, baseball, and wrestling, Black coaches are almost nonexistent.

And even those rare head coaching chances that are awarded Blacks are not what would be considered prime opportunities. Over the years, Blacks have headed football programs at Wake Forest, North Texas, New Mexico State, Long Beach State, Temple, and Nevada–LasVegas, all weak programs with very little tradition. Against such odds, it is difficult to build a successful track record as a head coach.

Although not discussed openly, many African-American coaches feel they are judged by a different standard than their White counterparts. They know that it is likely they will be given only one chance to succeed as a head coach. While White coaches such as Jim Harrick, Danny Ford, Johnny Majors, and Jerry Tarkanian, for example, received second chances to resurrect their careers, Black coaches such as Larry Finch and Wade Houston were "washed out of the system." Even if they continue to coach, most of them will never receive serious consideration for another head coaching job.

While the story of Blacks in coaching is disappointing, the tale regarding athletic administrators is sadder still. Only 3.6% of Division I athletic directors are African-American (Lapchick, 1996). Black associate and assistant athletic directors are also very few in number. According to the NCAA, only 4.5% of associate athletic director positions and 4.9% of assistant athletic director positions were held by African-Americans during the 1994 academic year (Lapchick, 1996). Almost no Division I senior woman administrator, development, marketing, business operations, game management, or overall administrative oversight positions are held by African-Americans. Even when minorities obtain jobs in college athletic departments, they are often pigeonholed into academic support and/or compliance positions that offer little room for advancement or professional growth.

Of course, college presidents and athletic directors claim they are unable to hire more Black coaches and administrators due to a shortage of viable African-American candidates. But according to the Black Coaches Association, its membership consisted of 2,500 members during the early 1990s (Lapchick, 1991), proof that there are plenty of ambitious and fully qualified Black candidates for coaching and administrative positions.

Thus, the question remains, with such a poor record regarding the hiring of minority coaches and administrators, coupled with the isolation and stereotyping of Black student-athletes, which in large part is perpetuated by those in the athletic establishment, how can athletics continue to justify its presence within our educational system on the grounds that it promotes integration and racial harmony? Despite the assertions of coaches and others in the athletic establishment, and the widespread public acceptance of those claims, the facts seem to indicate that this notion is more myth than reality.

What then can be done to help athletics realize its potential to promote integration?

PROMOTING MEANINGFUL INTEGRATION

It is no secret that coaches exert tremendous control over student-athletes' lives, both on and off the fields and courts. Strict structure and scheduling, coaches explain, are necessary for players to meet their significant athletic and academic obligations. Unfortunately, such control also contributes greatly to student-athletes' feelings of isolation, isolation that is particularly acute in the case of Black student-athletes. Consequently, there have been many calls to provide more opportunities for minority student-athletes to become more involved in campus and community life.

While such calls are appropriate and undoubtedly necessary, there is another aspect of the integration equation that often is overlooked. Specifically, coaches and athletic administrators must create opportunities for more interaction among student-athletes themselves. This notion became clear to me during a recent discussion with a few of my former African-American teammates. I was shocked to discover that most of us could not remember the names of many of our professors or any of the White students who lived in our dormitories. More significant, we realized that we had very little or no interaction with any of our White teammates off the field.

Despite what coaches might claim about successfully integrating their teams, simply because student-athletes are teammates does not mean that they respect and interact well with one another. Student-athletes are brought to campus as part of a large, diverse group and "forced" to interact with one another for purposes of functioning as an athletic unit. Off the fields and courts, however, student-athletes with similar backgrounds tend to migrate toward one another. Black players usually attend all-Black social functions, join all-Black organizations, and interact for the most part with other Black students. The same can be said of White student-athletes. Student-athletes must be forced out of their "racial comfort zones" and into an environment that will simulate the one that exists in the "real world." In other words, just because student-athletes are a part of an integrated athletic team, does not mean they do not need help in understanding and interacting with people of another race.

To that end, all student-athletes should be required to participate in diversity training workshops. Coaches and athletic administrators also should be required to participate in some of the workshops with their student-athletes. Such initiatives can help student-athletes to better communicate with, understand, and work with those who are different from them.

Coaches also can help the integration process by seeking ways to create off-the-field interaction between members of their teams. For example, during preseason football camp of my senior year, rather than allowing us to choose our own roommates, our head coach, Gerry Di-Nardo, made the room assignments, pairing every Black player with a White player. While most of us were displeased with this policy, I now understand what he was trying to accomplish. The lesson I learned while lying in bed at night after grueling two-a-day practices was that my roommate was no different than me. During those late night discussions, I realized that we were much more similar than I previously had thought.

CREATING OPPORTUNITY

As mentioned earlier, the athletic community's record regarding the hiring of Blacks and other minorities as coaches and administrators is disappointing, particularly considering the high percentage of Blacks in the revenue-generating sports of football and basketball. This issue is critical because it has a very direct effect on the educational and athletic experiences of Black student-athletes.

Role modeling plays a critical part in learning. That being the case, Black student-athletes must have the opportunity to interact with more athletic department employees of color. Seeing successful African-Americans in positions of influence enables Black student-athletes to envision themselves in such positions in the future. Therefore, the need to aggressively identify, hire, and develop more African-American coaches and administrators is obvious.

While there have been efforts to encourage institutions to identify and hire African-Americans, much more can be done. For example, it has been suggested that a third graduate assistant coaching position in football be created expressly for a minority candidate and, in basketball, that the restricted earnings coaching position be required to be filled by a minority. While such suggestions are well-intended, why must the only point of entry into an athletic department at a predominantly White institution be at the bottom of the coaching "totem pole"?

At the same time as athletic departments are identifying young candidates for these entry-level positions, they also should be considering the many experienced and well-qualified minority coaches at historically Black colleges and universities (HBCUs). In ignoring this vast talent pool, are athletic administrators suggesting that coaches at Black schools are less qualified than those at White institutions? There is the feeling among many Black coaches that if they accept a job at an HBCU, they may never get the opportunity to coach at a predominantly White institution, as in far too many cases, athletic directors or head coaches select White coaches from the high school level without even considering a coach from an HBCU. Similarly, if an administrator is capable of serving as an athletic director or assistant athletic director at an HBCU, isn't he or she qualified to serve in the same capacity at a predominantly White institution?

But there is more to addressing this issue than simply calling for improved hiring practices. One idea in particular bears mentioning. In an editorial printed in the *NCAA News*, Sean Frazier (1997) argued that the NCAA should recognize a position, similar to the senior woman administrator, for minority athletic administrators. The NCAA requires each institution to identify four key institutional administrators (president, athletic director, faculty athletic representative, and senior woman administrator) through which all Association business and communication are conducted. In the case of the senior woman administrator, this designation has done much to strengthen the position at the campus level. Frazier suggests, and correctly so, that a similar designation for minority administrators will serve to not only enhance the profile of minority administrators but also raise the level of awareness of issues that affect Black student-athletes.

With the all-out assault on affirmative action policies that is taking place on campuses today, Frazier's call will undoubtedly raise some eyebrows. Such concern, however, is unwarranted. Frazier is not suggesting a requirement that an institution hire a certain percentage of Black administrators. Simply because over 60% of basketball student-athletes are Black does not, for example, mean that 60% of coaches should be as well. Frazier is suggesting only that the NCAA, in an effort to strengthen the position of minority administrators on campus, designate a minority administrator through which NCAA issues and information would be directed. In short, if the NCAA can mandate that each college athletic department designate a senior woman administrator, why not a minority athletic administrator?

RE-ESTABLISHING COACHING PRIORITIES

I once overheard a head coach complaining that he had so many outside responsibilities that he could no longer "just coach." Those outside responsibilities he was referring to related to public relations, fund raising, recruiting, and the academic and personal development of his "players." While that coach was correct in his analysis of the proliferation of "outside" coaching responsibilities as it relates to the media and fund raising, his inclusion of academic responsibilities couldn't be further from the mark. If there is one coaching responsibility that can't ever change, it is that relating to the academic and personal development of the student-athlete. Academic responsibility is as fundamental a job component for the highly paid, full-time coach of today as it was for the English professor who coached on a part-time basis at the turn of the twentieth century. After all, coaches justify their place within the educational community on the basis that they are teachers and educators.

Coaches have come to view their academic responsibilities as being increasingly less important, primarily because of the development of comprehensive institutional academic support programs for student-athletes. Such programs include services ranging from tutoring and counseling, to diagnostic testing and career placement. As a result, many coaches simply "turn athletes over" to the academic support units upon their arrival on campus and then remove themselves from the academic process. Coaches abdicating their responsibility in this manner is simply unacceptable. The fact that such programs perform many of the hands-on academic services previously performed by coaches does not reduce, in any way, the responsibility not only to set an atmosphere in their programs that is conducive to academic achievement but also to take an active and very direct interest in the academic progress of each student-athlete. While coaches often resent this burden, citing the intense pressure to produce winning programs, there is simply no escaping the fact that they are usually the most influential people in the lives of their student-athletes. With such influence comes responsibility—responsibility that cannot be shirked under any circumstances.

Thus, a major challenge facing athletic departments and the coaching community is to understand the relationship between the student-athlete support program and coaches. The individual responsibilities of coaches, academic support staff, and the student-athletes themselves in the academic process must be clearly articulated and then executed. Coaches must understand fully that, other than student-athletes themselves, they play the most critical role in this process. Athletic directors, college presidents, and even principals at the high school level must not only articulate this responsibility to their coaches, but, more important, hold them accountable for this job performance standard. In short, educational institutions must take responsibility to ensure that all student-athletes have the opportunity to earn a meaningful education and lead quality lives both on and off the fields and courts of play.

As a former academic counselor for student-athletes, I understand that every youngster cannot be "saved." We certainly cannot guarantee that all student-athletes will graduate. We can, however, ensure that all student-athletes leave their campuses with the educational basics to help them integrate into and succeed in American society.

RAISING EXPECTATIONS

Finally, for athletic programs to fulfill their promise as a vehicle to promote the integration of Blacks and other minorities into mainstream society, the issue of expectations must be addressed. Simply put, if we expect Black student-athletes to become integrated into the student body or mainstream society, we must have the same expectations of them as we do of White athletes and students generally.

This is a difficult issue to address because it calls into question the validity of the widely proclaimed educational and socialization benefits of sport. Specifically, it is the deep-seated belief of many within the athletic establishment that Blacks are more gifted than Whites as athletes, but not as intelligent as Whites, that leads to lower academic and social expectations of Black student-athletes. While the athletic community claims to be "color blind," an argument can be made that it actually helps perpetuate this myth. How else can the well-documented dearth of Blacks in "decision-making" positions of quarterback in football or catcher in baseball, or the small number of athletic directors and head coaches in our colleges and universities, be explained? And could there be any relationship between levels of expectations and the significantly lower graduation rates of Black student-athletes as compared with White student-athletes?

As educators, we must have high expectations of all student-athletes, both on and off the fields and courts. Those expectations must be identical for both Black and White student-athletes. Student-athletes will perform up to their expected level of success. We must hold student-athletes accountable for their actions. We must stop "baby-sitting" them. We must stop "fixing" all their problems. How often has a coach or athletic administrator made a phone call to a professor to change a grade, a police officer to dismiss a charge, or a booster to provide a "cush" summer job?

While there is a fine line between meeting the unique needs of student-athletes and "coddling" them, our tendency as coaches and athletic administrators is to make their decisions, fix their problems, and do their work. All this in the name of keeping them eligible and focused on their athletic development. Such an approach, however, is educationally irresponsible as it does nothing to instill in youngsters the sense of personal accountability essential for success in life. In sum, expectations are important and we must stop expecting less from Black student-athletes.

TURNING MYTH INTO REALITY

One of the most fundamental issues facing our country is the challenge of multiculturalism. As our population becomes more diverse, it will become increasingly important for people of different races to work together to achieve common goals. And the role our educational system must play in promoting racial equality and tolerance is vital.

Despite its uneven record on matters of diversity, athletics, if used effectively, can be a powerful tool to promote tolerance, teamwork, and multiculturalism. But to fully realize athletics' enormous potential in this regard will require commitment on the part of coaches, teachers, faculty, and administrators at all levels. Negative stereotypes of the Black student-athlete must be discredited, academic expectations must be raised, attitudes must be changed, and genuine opportunities to tap the tremendous leadership potential of Black coaches and administrators must be created.

Until such fundamental change occurs, athletic programs that are conducted as part of our educational institutions will continue to contribute to the racial isolation and educational disenfranchisement of Blacks. In other words, it is time to turn the myth of sport's power to transcend racial barriers into reality.

REFERENCES

Blauvelt, H., & Carey, J. (1995, August 2). Black coaches still find doors closed. *USA Today*, p. 3-C.

Fish, M. (1997a, March 2). Black football players source of cheap labor for schools. *The Atlanta Journal-Constitution*, p. E9.

Fish, M. (1997b, March 2). Where is the justice? *The Atlanta Journal-Constitution*, p. E9.

Frazier, S. (1997, December 15). SWA-type position needed for minorities [Letter to the editor]. *NCAA News*, p. 4.

Lapchick, R. E. (1991). *Five minutes to midnight: Race and sport in the 1990s.* New York: Madison Books.

Lapchick, R. E. (1996, January 8). Race still most pressing ethical issue in college sports. *The Dallas Morning News,* p. 3B.

National Collegiate Athletic Association (1996a). *1996 NCAA Division I graduation rates report.* Overland Park, KS: Author.

National Collegiate Athletic Association. (1996b, December 9). Study shows graduation rates up, minority enrollment on rebound. *NCAA News,* pp. 1, 8.

Orr, J. (1969). *The black athlete: His story in American history.* New York: Lion Press.

Spencer, S. (1994, November 8). Story for sale. *Seattle Post Intelligencer,* pp. D1, D4.

8

The Myth of Athletics and Educational Opportunity

Darren Bilberry

When James Meredith attempted to enroll as the first Black student to attend the University of Mississippi, he was met with stiff resistance from all corners of the state. The resulting 2-day outbreak of mob violence was not an uncommon reaction to integration efforts in 1962. Eventually justice prevailed and Meredith was provided the opportunity to fulfill his dream of equal educational opportunity. It was the tremendous courage and commitment of Meredith and many others, both Black and White, often against seemingly insurmountable forces, that pried open the door of educational opportunity.

The thousands who worked to advance the educational interests of Blacks did so at great personal risk. Many paid the ultimate price for their belief in the importance of access to quality education and its critical influence on all integration efforts. They knew Blacks could never achieve equal social and economic justice without equal educational opportunity.

Sport has long been portrayed as one of America's most progressive institutions in matters of race. This belief, perpetuated largely by coaches, athletic administrators, and the media, began to gain widespread acceptance in the 1950s. In 1956, John Lardner, a sports columnist for *Newsweek* wrote that "race equality in baseball and in jazz music has done more than anything else to improve the climate for integration in America" (p. 85). *The New York Times* offered its take on the role of sport in integration in a 1959 editorial: "There has been no one channel of understanding that has been better than that of sports. It has proved that most problems can be solved in the right spirit" (p. IV 8).

Athletics continually is cited as a shining example of how people of various races and creeds work together for a common cause. More specifically, athletics is cast as one of the most critical and effective tools" for providing educational opportunity for thousands of African-Americans. Beyond the fields of play, however, it becomes obvious that these claims are largely untrue, simply another myth promoted by the sports establishment to justify its ill-conceived relationship with our country's educational system. To portray high school, and particularly college, athletics as institutions that are committed to providing meaningful educational opportunity for millions of Black athletes is to shame the memory and sacrifices of Meredith and the thousands of others who put their lives on the line for their belief in true educational opportunity. Despite idealized notions to the contrary, the integration of high school and college athletic teams has had very little to do with providing meaningful educational opportunities to Blacks, but everything to do with winning and money.

EDUCATIONAL OPPORTUNITY OR ATHLETIC SERVITUDE?

In his 1991 book *Five Minutes to Midnight: Race and Sport in the 1990s,* Richard Lapchick documents two occurrences that clearly demonstrate the motivation behind integrating once all-White athletic teams. After Sam Cunningham scored three touchdowns to help the University of Southern California rout the University of Alabama football team, Paul "Bear" Bryant reportedly walked off the field muttering, "He just did more for integration in the South in 60 minutes than Martin Luther King did in 20 years." The crowd, after witnessing Cunningham's dominant performance, allegedly besieged the Alabama coaches with cries of, "Get us one! Get us one!" They did so—the very next season. Four years after losing to a team (Texas Western) with five Black starters in the 1966 NCAA Championship game, Adolph Rupp, despite his openly racist attitude, brought his first Black basketball player to the University of Kentucky. The coaches of both schools were correct in assuming that to stay competitive, they had no choice but to integrate their rosters.

    Members of the athletic establishment argue that regardless of the original motivation, sport has done more to improve race relations in America than virtually any other institution. "Just look at the fields of play," they cry. "Where else in America have Blacks had such opportunity to compete on equal footing?"

    While it may be true that colleges and high schools have, for the most part, achieved integration on the fields of play, the issue is not the athletic opportunities that have been afforded Blacks, but the educational opportunities that have not. It is only through access to meaningful educational opportunity that genuine integration can occur off the fields of play. On this front, our educational institutions have fallen far short of their self-proclaimed integrationist accomplishments.

As proof that equal opportunity for Blacks exists only on the fields of play, one needs only to look at the small number of Blacks in coaching and decision-making positions throughout the athletic establishment. According to the *NCAA Minority Opportunities and Interests Committee's Four-Year Study of Race Demographics of Member Institutions*, excluding historically Black colleges and universities, in 1993–94, less than 4% of NCAA directors of athletics and only 7% of NCAA head coaches were Black. In the revenue-producing sports of Division I football and basketball, only 10% of head coaches were Black (NCAA, 1994).

These shortfalls are particularly stark considering the high percentage of minority student's participating in athletics. According to the *1996 NCAA Division I Graduation Rates Report*, 24% of scholarship student-athletes entering Division I athletic programs from the 1986–87 through 1989–90 academic years were African-American. The numbers are particularly high in football (44%), men's basketball (59%), and women's basketball (34%) (NCAA, 1996).

These disappointing statistics reflect the end result of a system that continues to deny genuine educational opportunity to Blacks at almost every turn.

A DIFFERENT SET OF EXPECTATIONS

The most pressing issue regarding race in athletic programs conducted within our country's educational systems has nothing to do with anything that occurs on the fields of play. Rather, it is the myth that athletics has been used to provide Black youth with educational opportunity. Ironically, the greatest force working against student-athletes being able to transform athletic achievement into educational advancement are the low expectations and resultant behavior of the very people who promote athletics as a provider of meaningful educational opportunity for thousands of African-Americans—coaches and other members of the athletic and educational establishment.

Black student-athletes routinely are admitted to colleges with lower academic credentials than the general student body. While most universities have special admissions criteria through which students who do not meet regular admissions standards can be admitted, it is no secret that at most schools that sponsor major college athletics, a disproportionately large number of those "special admits" are Black student-athletes in the high-visibility sports of football and basketball.

According to the NCAA, about 3 percent of all students enter as special admissions, while more than 20 percent of football and basketball players enter under this program. Since there are so many football and basketball players who are black, one might assume that a very large percentage of special admits playing those sports are black (Lapchick, 1991, p. 229).

Once on campus, Black student-athletes often are held to lower academic expectations than are other students, while what is expected of them athletically is higher. Athletic time demands are often excessive, and the control exerted over almost every phase of student-athletes' lives by coaches intent on maximizing athletic performance severely limits the ability to sample the broad social, cultural, and educational opportunities that are a part of a well-rounded college education.

Dr. John Harris is the former Dean of the College of Education and is currently Professor of Administration and Educational Law at the University of Kentucky. He is also a scholar in African-American studies, speaking often of the double jeopardy that Black student-athletes face regarding academic expectations. He suggests that

stereotypical attitudes of the predominantly white faculty are generated by the assumption that most black athletes are underqualified special admits. Because mandatory athletic responsibilities take time away from academic endeavors, it is widely believed that the student-athlete's only academic purpose is to achieve the bare minimum required to remain eligible to compete athletically (personal interview, March 10, 1998).

THE REAL STORY

What about all those stories of White coaches who have "rescued" Black student-athletes from the ghetto? In most cases, we never hear how the story ends. In my position as academic advisor, I spoke often to Black athletes about their collegiate experience. One conversation in particular stands out. After transferring to the university from a junior college, this young man was never able to fulfill the academic requirements to become eligible. He explained that because he had no money and poor grades in high school, he never considered attending college. After he displayed an extraordinary amount of athletic talent as a junior, coaches came calling as if college was suddenly the natural next step in his life. For 17 years no one had shown an interest in his education or his future. In fact, he could not even imagine life after age 20. To him, being on a college campus was like being on "another planet." In his case, he might as well have been.

A student who reads at only the grade school level is not academically prepared or qualified to attend college. What coaches often fail to realize, or simply refuse to acknowledge, is that even if that student-athlete can run the 40-yard dash in 4.5 seconds and bench press 300 pounds, he still is not prepared for college. If he can run the 40-yard dash in 4.5 seconds and bench press 300 pounds, but can read only at the grade school level, why is it that once he arrives on campus, he is required to spend more time improving his speed and strength than his ability to read?

"Even if he does not graduate,"argues the coach, "he is better off for the experience." What experience? Despite the fact that such students might not be academically prepared or motivated, they are, like most young adults, very perceptive. They understand why they are advised to take specific classes with professors who are "friends" of the athletic program. They know why they are "encouraged" to enroll in certain majors. They understand that the illegal "incentives" they sometimes receive, their celebrity status, and the temporary shield from overt racism that they experience usually end along with their athletic eligibility. More than one Black student-athlete has stated it quite bluntly: "I know that if I were not an athlete, most of these people would not care about me. I'd be just another 'nigger' to most of them."

This shift from overt to covert racist attitudes toward Black athletes presents particularly challenging conflicts. Despite the fact that young Black athletes are well aware that they are being used for their athletic talents, it is difficult for them not to embrace their celebrity status. The conflict between hero worship at the expense of exploitation makes it difficult for them to discern between what is real and what is superficial in regard to their acceptance into the mainstream White community. Complicating the matter is their unwillingness to talk openly regarding their feelings because of fears of losing their celebrity status, scholarship, and any future athletic opportunity in professional sports. When their eligibility is up and the benefits they enjoyed as athletes are cut off, they continue to remain silent because they do not want to subject themselves to the humiliation and embarrassment of admitting that they were exploited by the system.

Fred Buttler is one of the few Black athletes who has been willing to share his story. Even though he was unable to read beyond the second-grade level, not only was Fred passed through grade school, but he was permitted to skip eighth grade entirely because his high school coach was eager to get him on the varsity football team. He maintained a C average throughout high school, junior college, and college. Soon after his eligibility was up, he flunked out of school. In retrospect, Fred seemed well aware of what was happening to him, but his belief that a career in the NFL would secure his financial future prevented him from speaking out (Lapchick, 1991, p. 256).

Fred Buttler's case illustrates that the notion that Black student-athletes from impoverished backgrounds are provided a genuine, meaningful educational opportunity simply because the athletic department is paying the bills is often an illusion. In their 1994 book, *Lessons of the Locker Room*, Andrew Miracle and C. Roger Rees explain the nature of this illusion as follows:

> High school sport may open doors to college for athletes, but it does little to guarantee that they will walk out of those doors four years later with a degree. If athletes are deficient in academic skills in high school, they are not likely to gain those academic skills at college. Indeed they are much more likely to major in academic eligibility at college and take courses only to maintain the required GPA. In this situation the only chance of a pay-off is a pro contract, and the odds against this are very great. (p. 148)

But what of all of the "success" stories—the student-athletes who graduate or make millions playing professionally? Certainly, student-athletes who earn a degree are better off than those who do not. But the question concerning whether they have been allowed to reach their full potential as students remains. Did they have the opportunity to earn their degree of choice, or was their major selection dictated by what their athletic commitments would allow them to pursue? With the job market, as well as graduate and professional schools, being so competitive, is "barely making it" going to be enough? Was "educational opportunity" a reality or an illusion? As for playing professionally, the chances are so remote that in practical terms it is not much of an opportunity at all. Yet, despite the obvious benefits of a college degree versus the unrealistic dreams of a career in professional sports, the goals and expectations of Black student-athletes relate more to winning and athletic development than to education—and those dreams are fueled primarily by coaches.

THE PROBLEMS FILTER DOWN

High schools are not immune to these problems. Like universities, they recruit athletes not to provide an educational opportunity, but for their athletic potential. High school coaches are not immune to sacrificing academic principles in the name of winning at any cost. And gifted athletes continue to be passed along from grade to grade regardless of whether they meet the academic qualifications to pass.

James Webb has been a high school football and track coach in Kentucky for the past 7 years. He has seen firsthand, far too many young Black student-athletes neglect their education because they believe they will be the next Michael Jordan. Webb also has seen the surrounding community—parents, coaches, athletic directors, the media—applaud these youngsters for their athletic accomplishments while turning their heads away from the youngsters' self-defeating attitude regarding education. He has witnessed parents permitting their sons and daughters, based on coaches' recruiting, to switch schools to find the best athletic program with little concern regarding academic implications. He is most shocked at the practice of "redshirting," a tactic that once was reserved for college athletic programs. He says,

> "Even if a child is progressing well academically, overzealous parents, often at the urging of coaches, will have their children repeat a grade to allow them to further develop athletically before beginning competition at the high school level. These parents, particularly those of black high school athletes, have fallen victim to the myth, perpetuated by many coaches and athletic administrators, that sports, rather than education, is the key to life-long success" (personal interview, March, 1, 1998).

Lapchick (1991) supports Webb's claim and provides even more detailed evidence that high school sports are adopting the "win-at-all-costs" philosophy of intercollegiate sports.

> Many teenagers have already gone through a recruiting process to get to high school. Coaches even help a prospect's family relocate nearer to the school. High school teachers reportedly pass illiterate players to keep them eligible. The seemingly easy ride to the top has begun. In 1983, less than 100 of 16,000 high school districts required a "C" average to participate in sport.... Between 25 and 30 percent of high school senior football and basketball players reportedly leave school functionally illiterate. (p. 218)

As long as Black student-athletes are viewed as a separate and unequal group, with less expected of them academically and socially, the myth that football fields and basketball courts are the keys to future economic and personal success will continue to be perpetuated.

MAKING OPPORTUNITY A REALITY

In response to concerns regarding the academic welfare of college student-athletes, athletic departments began in the 1970s to hire tutors and academic advisors. While at first designed for the sole purpose of keeping athletes eligible, over the years the academic support services offered to athletes have expanded to include increased tutoring budgets, more study space, computer labs, career counseling, and job placement services. The growth of such programs is evidence of an increased commitment to the development of the student-athlete, not only athletically, but academically and socially as well.

In an effort to ensure that student-athletes' needs are being met, the NCAA has taken steps to allow student-athletes more input into athletic department decision-making processes. For example, the NCAA now mandates that athletic departments form student-athlete advisory committees and conduct a formalized exit interview program. Athletic departments should welcome student-athlete feedback, because open and honest communication between administrators, coaches, and student-athletes is crucial to turning the opportunity of an athletic scholarship into the reality of an education.

While the appropriation of more resources for academic support programs and initiatives to increase communication are certainly steps in the right direction, there must be a new philosophy regarding the education and overall development of student-athletes. All the academic support services in the world will not benefit a student-athlete who arrives on campus illiterate. Nor will they benefit those student-athletes who are not given adequate time by their coaches to utilize these resources. To ensure that they are in a position to take advantage of the educational opportunities presented by an athletic scholarship, athletes must understand that it is education, not athletics, that offers the best path to future success. This message must be stressed from the first time the athlete steps onto a playing field or court as a youth-league participant and continually re-emphasized until he or she graduates from college. The responsibility to not only promote this message, but also follow through with actions that support it, rests firmly on the shoulders of coaches and athletic administrators at all levels.

Coaches must temper their "win-at-all-costs" philosophies and place a higher priority on the academic and personal development of their student-athletes. They must demand the same level of high academic achievement and commitment to education that they do for athletics. Youth coaches must support the equal participation of all the children in their programs rather than catering to the handful of 8-year-olds who show athletic promise. High school coaches, teachers, and administrators must not stand idly by while their best player is "passed along" from grade to grade regardless of whether he or she meets academic qualifications. College coaches must reconnect with their responsibilities as educators by spending less time selling the products they endorse and more time promoting the importance and value of education. Athletic directors must find the courage to evaluate coaches based on their ability and success as educators rather than exclusively on their win/loss records.

Members of the athletic establishment must take responsibility for implementing, rather than simply talking about, these types of fundamental changes. Without such commitment, their claims of educational opportunity through athletics will continue to ring hollow.

COURAGE FOR A HIGHER CAUSE

In the spring of 1997, the University of Kentucky hired a Black head basketball coach. As expected, the sports establishment used this hiring as an opportunity to further promote athletics as a powerful player in our country's civil rights landscape. Many compared the courage of coaches and other athletic leaders to that of civil rights leaders such as Medgar Evers, James Meredith, and Fannie Lou Hamer. While the actions of such athletic leaders are important, likening them to Medgar Evers and the thousands who died in the civil rights struggle blatantly discredits the legacies of the civil rights leaders. One cause was for the sake of justice, the other for winning ballgames.

A more valid connection between athletics and the struggle for civil rights would be made by telling the story of John Carlos and Tommie Smith's protest at the 1968 Olympic Games over the general reign of terror Blacks were experiencing in America. At the height of their athletic achievement, precisely when they had the most to lose, these athletes made a courageous stand, not unlike the one made by Meredith. They refused to accept America's conditional and temporary adulation of them as athletes; they refused to simply accept the kernel of false athletic "opportunity" and demanded real opportunity and justice. Ironically, the same athletic establishment that is so quick to promote athletics as a shining example of racial tolerance, met and continues to view these athletes' black-fisted salute of protest with scorn and hatred.

Modern-day Black athletes, and for that matter Black coaches and administrators, should take note of the actions of Carlos, Smith, and Meredith. Everyone associated with the athletic enterprise, from the peewee leagues to the major college level, bears responsibility for helping to transform athletic opportunity into educational reality. It is, however, Black athletes, coaches, and administrators themselves who bear a greater share of that responsibility.

The most obvious, and indeed radical, measure to prompt more meaningful action on the part of the athletic establishment would be a boycott. It has been suggested on more than one occasion that athletes banding together to postpone or delay the start of the NCAA men's basketball championship game might be the only way to get the college athletic community to seriously consider the issues that affect athletes. That is not the approach that is being advocated here. Meaningful change can occur using a more measured, three-pronged approach.

First, Black athletes must become more informed regarding the issues that so greatly affect them, particularly the practices and attitudes that deny them access to meaningful educational opportunity. More specifically, they must begin to educate themselves regarding their rights. For example, in 1995, in response to increasing calls to address student-athlete concerns, the NCAA (1997) adopted six "Principles of Student-Athlete Welfare." Of particular note are two principles, one, the right for a well-balanced, "overall educational experience," and the second, outlining the institution's "responsibility to maintain an environment that values cultural diversity and gender equity" (p. 3). While this legislation looks good on paper, it lacks backbone in the form of student-athletes knowing that they have these rights and then coupling that knowledge with their leverage as highly visible athletes to force meaningful change in these areas.

Second, the Black Coaches Association must initiate outreach programs designed to join forces with Black athletes and administrators at all levels to better coordinate and advance the issues that affect them. It is only by presenting a coordinated, unified front that the concerns identified in this chapter will be addressed in a meaningful manner. Broad-based strategies, educational efforts, and communication initiatives must be developed and implemented using a network that must include college and high school athletes.

Third, Black athletes, coaches, and administrators themselves must take responsibility for changing the educational environment for Black athletes of all ages. Specifically, we must go beyond simplistic calls for Black athletes to be "positive" role models. As discussed by Todd Crosset in Chapter 3, there are significant problems with expecting athletes to be educational role models. Regardless, Black athletes can have an impact on the lives of others by being advocates of social change. In fact, the "positive" in role model is in the eyes of the beholder. It is doubtful that the White athletic establishment would consider as a "positive" role model a strong-willed, outspoken Black athlete who called attention to the covert racism, educational discrimination, and illusion of educational opportunity through sports. Such a social activist would more likely be considered a malcontent or troublemaker.

Rather than worrying about image and role-model status, Black athletes, as well as coaches and administrators, must become more aggressive in using their high visibility and access to the media to bring these educational concerns to light. Rather than continuing to accept the status quo, rather than being content with simply the opportunity to play ball on national television, Black athletes must want more—namely, genuine educational opportunity. They must be willing to speak out and stand up for it. Black coaches and administrators must do the same.

Stepping forward to create the change necessary for more Black athletes to realize meaningful educational opportunity through athletics will take courage. It will take courage not unlike that displayed by John Carlos and Tommie Smith—courage to risk personal comfort and gain for the sake of real opportunity for others. Only then will the problems facing all Blacks, not simply Black athletes, receive the attention and concrete actions necessary for their resolution. Only then will the myth of educational opportunity for Blacks through athletics become a reality. Simply put, James Meredith risked his life for equal educational opportunity for Blacks, not for the false hopes and dreams of athletic stardom.

REFERENCES

Lapchick, R. (1991). *Five minutes to midnight: Race and sport in the 1990s.* Lanham, MD: Madison Books.

Lardner, J. (1956, April 2). The old emancipator—1. *Newsweek,* p. 85.

Miracle, A. W., Jr. & Rees, C. R. (1994). *Lessons of the locker room: The myth of school sports.* Amherst, NY: Prometheus Books.

National Collegiate Athletic Association. (1994). *NCAA Minority Opportunities and Interests Committee's Four-year study of race demographics of member institutions.* Overland Park, KS: Author.

National Collegiate Athletic Association. (1996). *1996 NCAA Division I graduation rates report.* Overland Park, KS: Author.

National Collegiate Athletic Association. (1997). *1997–98 NCAA manual.* Overland Park, KS: Author.

New York Times. (1959, May 31). [Editorial] p. IV8.

Webb, J. (1998, March 1). [Personal interview].

9

Women in Sports: Seeking Balance

Darlene Bailey

One of the most talked about issues in education during the past decade has been that of equal opportunity for women in athletics. From the youth to the collegiate levels, coaches, athletic administrators, and other educational leaders have been struggling to meet the provisions of Title IX of the 1972 Educational Amendment Act, which mandates that educational institutions receiving federal support provide women equal opportunity as it relates to athletics.

Unquestionably, the passage of Title IX has led to a significant increase in participation opportunities for women and girls in sports. While many have cited this increase as a sign that they are well on their way to achieving equity in the scholastic and collegiate sports arenas, women continue to be denied the single most important opportunity relating to athletics. Because women are woefully underrepresented in key decision-making positions such as athletic director, coach, business manager, and commissioner, they continue to be denied the opportunity to utilize their unique talents, perspective, and approach to leadership to work with men to influence the future of athletics in this country. It is the opportunity to contribute to the decision-making process that will shape the future of not only women's athletics, but men's as well,—its structure, philosophy, and programs. This represents the most critical and far-reaching issue in the gender equity struggle.

MODELING AFTER THE MEN?

While the lack of participation opportunities, quality of those opportunities, and salary equity are all important, the issue that has the most potential to inflict long-term damage to women's athletics is the prevailing

Sports in School: The Future of an Institution. Copyright © 2000 by Teachers College, Columbia University. All rights reserved. ISBN 0-8077-3970-7 (paper), ISBN 0-8077-3971-5 (cloth). Prior to photocopying items for classroom use, please contact the Copyright Clearance Center, Customer Service, 222 Rosewood Drive, Danvers, MA 01923, USA, telephone (508) 750-8400.

mind-set that to be "successful," women's sports programs must mirror men's, specifically, the high-profile, revenue-generating sports of Division I football, basketball, baseball, and hockey.

Many women coaches and administrators subscribe to the belief that women's programs should be shaped according to the men's model. This is understandable because women who have worked their way into the existing decision-making structure have had only male models of behavior and attitudes to emulate. Further, the current men's athletic model is viewed as the only "successful" model in existence. But it is precisely this concept of "success," as it applies to athletic programs conducted within educational institutions, that must be reconsidered if sport is to reach its potential to contribute to the broad goals and mission of those institutions. By all indications, women are uniquely qualified to provide the type of leadership necessary to meet these educational challenges.

As articulated by various authors throughout this book, when defined by the current standards of revenue generated, television appearances made, and championships won, it is arguable whether these high-profile Division I men's programs are, in fact, "successful"—at least as applied to athletics conducted within an educational setting. But the purpose of this chapter is not to dwell on the negative aspects of college sports. Most of what transpires within our athletic programs, both men's and women's, is positive. Such grave concerns about the overall administration of athletics, however, cannot be ignored. It is therefore ironic that women's programs continue to be shaped according to a model that, many argue, is seriously flawed.

As long as men continue to dominate the key decision-making positions in the newly emerging women's sports structure, women's programs run the very real risk of becoming nothing more than an imitation of men's athletics—bigger but not better, just alike rather than something special, the usual rather than unique. Simply put, with men holding virtually all of the major decision-making jobs in women's athletics, women continue to play sports by men's rules. But are men's rules the best rules, particularly as they apply to athletics conducted within an educational setting?

This is not to suggest that there should be a division in the administration of athletic programs, with women administering women's programs and men running men's. Rather, the purpose of this chapter is to call for increased opportunity for women to join the men and women already in place who are administering all athletic programs—women and men working together to shape emerging women's programs and redefine existing men's programs.

As the corporate community is beginning to discover, a growing body of research suggests that women bring a different perspective and approach to corporate offices and boardrooms, one that places more emphasis on cooperation and participation as opposed to strict competition. Similar to the way the business community is benefiting from a more diverse corporate decision-making structure and philosophy, so too can our athletic programs.

The challenge facing educational administrators at all levels is to develop women's sports programs that incorporate the positive, while tempering the negative, aspects of existing revenue-producing men's programs. The critical nature of this venture cannot be overemphasized because it is the rapidly emerging women's sports culture and structure that represent, perhaps, the final chance for athletic programs to refocus priorities in a way that will allow them to contribute in more direct and meaningful ways to the educational goals of our schools and colleges.

BEYOND PARTICIPATION

Those who have argued that girls are not interested in sports cannot ignore the fact that when opportunities for participation have been created, the response has been overwhelming. The main reason girls and women did not play sports prior to the mid-1970s is that opportunities simply did not exist.

According to the National Federation of State High School Associations, there were 294,015 participants in interscholastic teams for girls in 1971–72 compared with 3,666,917 boy participants, representing only 7.4% of total participants. By 1994–95 the number of girl participants had increased to 2,240,461, 33.1% of the total (Corbin & Pangrazi, 1997).

In 1996, the average number of women's teams offered per school at the collegiate level for all divisions was 7.5, up from 5.6 in 1977 (Acosta & Carpenter, 1996). The number of female participants at the collegiate level increased as well. The 1997 NCAA Gender Equity Study Summary of Results reported that the average number of female participants per Division I institution had increased from 112 in 1992 to 130 in 1997. In 1992, the average student-athlete population at an NCAA Division I institution was 69% male, 31% female. By 1997, females accounted for 37% of the total (NCAA, 1997). These numbers clearly indicate that, in the case of athletic participation opportunities for girls and women, if it is built, they will come.

Unfortunately, many discussions of Title IX and what must be done to promote gender equity stop at the issue of participation. Some of the most glaring inequities, however, have little to do with participation.

Many female athletes are not receiving equitable opportunities for coaching, nor are they receiving equivalent supplies, equipment, uniforms, facilities, and travel accommodations.

For example, according to the 1997 NCAA Gender Equity Study, in 1992, women received 17% of total recruiting dollars. In 1997, women received only 27% of the total. Women received only 38% of scholarship dollars (up from 31%) over the same 5-year period. Improvements were less impressive in the areas of coaches' salaries. In 1992, head coaches of women's sports received 36% of head coaches' salaries. In 1997, this figure was 40%. Assistant coaches' salaries for women's sports were only 18% of the total for all assistant coaches in 1992. In 1997, women received 24% of the total.

In one area there was no improvement over the 5-year period of the study. In 1992, women's sports received an average of 23% of the operating expenses for all Division I institutions, while men's sports received 77%. This ratio was identical in 1997. In fact, a smaller number of male athletes continued to receive the same percentage of the operating expenditures (NCAA, 1997). A closer look at the NCAA data indicates that the operating expenses per athlete in 1992 were $2,448.82 for men and $1,598.91 for women. In 1997, these figures had increased to $5,155.30 per male athlete and $2,604.61 per female athlete, a 211% increase in spending for male athletes compared with only a 163% increase for female athletes. This is particularly disturbing given that this 5-year period has been recognized as one of the most progressive for the female college athlete.

Rather than dwelling on the participation issue, it is critical that higher education institutions, government agencies, and other interested parties "take care of" those girls and women already playing sports. To do this may mean taking a long, hard look at the "sacred cow" of big-time college athletics—football. While football cannot be the scapegoat for college athletics' slow compliance with Title IX, the expenses allocated to maintain football are, in many cases, exorbitant. To achieve gender equity, critical scrutiny of the amount of resources allocated to football is essential.

Even at institutions without football, gender equity concerns abound. In 1993, a Title IX complaint was filed against Wichita State University. The U.S. Office of Civil Rights (OCR) report, released in 1995, found discriminatory practices in virtually every program area, including participation and scholarship opportunities. Wichita State does not have a football program and is not the only institution that would be out of compliance, even if football were taken out of the calculations. Since 1995, Wichita State has taken dramatic steps and dedicated considerable resources to a 3-year plan to bring the athletic program into compliance with Title IX in all areas found to be deficient by OCR (Wichita State University, 1995).

BREAKING THE CYCLE OF INDIFFERENCE

The lack of women's representation in administrative and coaching has been well documented. In 1972, when Title IX was enacted, 90% of women's teams were coached by females. In 1996, it was reported that 47.7% of the coaches of women's teams were female, down from 49.4% in 1994. There were 209 more jobs available in 1996 for coaches of women's NCAA teams in all divisions. However, the number of women holding those jobs actually decreased by nine. In 1996, women held 61.1% of the paid assistant coaching positions for women's sport teams (Acosta & Carpenter, 1996). Less than 2% of coaches of men's teams are women. At the high school level, as of 1990, more than 40% of girls' teams were coached by men, but only 2% of boys' teams were coached by women (Equal Employment Opportunity Commission, 1997).

Only 18.5% of women's athletic programs in the NCAA are headed by a female administrator. This is a decrease from 21% in 1994. The decline is mostly the product of a decline in the number of females who headed all-women programs in Division I (Acosta & Carpenter, 1996). Most Division I men's and women's athletic programs are now combined, with a single director. In November 1997, Vivian Fuller became the Director of Athletics at Tennessee State University, the only African-American woman to head a Division I athletics program and one of only seven women directing programs with football teams. Of the 986 NCAA members, only 19, less than 2%, have females running combined men's and women's programs (Wenninger, 1997). There are no females involved at all in 23.8% of women's programs. While overall there are more women in administrative jobs (35.9%) than ever before, most are not in the key decision-making positions of athletic director, assistant athletic director for business or operations, or conference commissioner.

The small number of athletic directors who are women is disturbing, especially when coupled with the other major influential group of administrators involved in college athletics—conference commissioners. The 1997–98, Collegiate Commissioners Association Directory, which includes all NCAA Division I institutions, listed 32 member conferences. Only three of the commissioners were women. There were none in the Division I-A conferences with major college football programs (CCA, 1997). The percentage of women in other sports organizations is similarly small. The International Olympic Committee comprises 99 men and only seven women. Between 1990 and 1996, of the 42 new appointments made, only two were women (Davenport, 1996). And when it comes to "spreading the word" about women's athletics through the media, there are not many women to carry the torch. Women make up only 11.9% of the full-time sports information directors in all divisions of the NCAA (Acosta & Carpenter, 1996). Thus, it comes as no surprise that according to *College Sports* magazine, the list of "Fifty Most Influential People in College Sports in 1996" included only six women (Coakley, 1998).

While progress in the area of participation is evident, the same cannot be said for administrative and coaching positions. If the past is any indication, we can expect progress to be painfully slow. At the rate changes have occurred since the mid-1980s, we can expect that women will make up only 20% of athletic directors by the year 2010, and a mere 4% in Division I.

Meeting the letter and intent of Title IX will require commitment, creativity, persistence, and hard work. One needs to look no further than the fact that during the 20 years from the passage of Title IX in 1972, there was virtually no progress on the gender equity front. The commitment, creativity, and hard work needed for change simply were not displayed by those in positions to make a difference—mostly male athletic administrators and coaches. For this reason, it is absolutely critical that more women be provided the opportunity to develop and guide college athletic programs. Female coaches and athletic administrators undoubtedly will have the most creative and committed approach to meeting the gender equity challenge. Simply put, more women deserve the opportunity to break this cycle of gender equity indifference.

BUILDING A NEW MODEL

Women's sports, especially team sports, are always compared with the men's and always come up short. It has been said that women's basketball games will never be as good as men's until the women can dunk consistently. It has been said that softball will never be as good as baseball because women cannot hit the ball as far, and women's track not as interesting as men's because women don't run as fast. The standards for achievement have been set by men. Popular culture has determined that because women cannot match these standards, women's sports are not interesting to watch (Coakley, 1998). But there is far more to college and high school sports than the games themselves. After all, these athletic programs are part of academic institutions, justified in large part on the educational benefits that accrue to participants.

While the inclusion of women's sports by the NCAA has been very positive in terms of increased participation and dollars dedicated to women's programs, it is interesting to wonder how different college athletics might be had the tables been turned and had the Association of Intercollegiate Athletics for Women included men's sports. Perhaps education would still be a central focus of athletic participation. Perhaps sports participation would be more inclusive. And perhaps we would not be questioning why some forms of sport are out of control.

These questions illustrate why the representation of women in key decision-making positions is more than simply a matter of equity and equality. It is an opportunity to shape the future. It may be the last chance to structure athletic programs that hold true to their educational purposes—programs that place paramount importance on the academic and personal development of the student-athletes and contribute in more direct and meaningful ways to the educational institutions of which they are a part.

If more women were provided an opportunity to work with men to shape athletic programs, what might they look like? What principles would they be based on and what values would they promote? Could such programs increase the emphasis on the academic and personal development of our sons and daughters? Could such programs fit more comfortably into the fabric of the educational institutions of which they are a part? The answer is a resounding, "Yes!"

CREATING OPPORTUNITIES

Before women will be able to exert more influence within the college athletic community, there must be more of them in positions to do so. While the NCAA and its institutions are making strides in creating and highlighting the need for increased opportunities for women in athletics, the process will require an ongoing effort by both men and women. Change of the magnitude necessary to ensure equal opportunity for women will take time and much work. Following are some suggestions to help in that process.

1. *Aggressive Identification, Recruiting, and Retention Efforts.* The college athletic community must become more aggressive in identifying and attracting quality women into the profession through an expansion of

graduate assistantships, internships, and administrative fellowship and scholarship opportunities. Once well-qualified women are in the "pipeline," they must be nurtured and developed to the point where they can succeed in the field. To this end, the importance of mentoring cannot be overestimated. Women entering the profession must be encouraged to identify mentors, both men and women, and then be allowed to aggressively tap into their experience. Conversely, those already established in the field, both men and women, must assume more mentoring responsibility. Mentoring takes time and effort. If we say we are committed to providing high-quality opportunities to women in athletics, veteran coaches and administrators must assume more personal responsibility for passing along their knowledge and expertise to the next generation of college athletic leaders.

2. *Creating a More Supportive Work Environment.* As in the corporate world, college athletics must become more accepting and supportive of the family obligations of both men and women. For example, increased work schedule flexibility, including liberal family leave policies, must be embraced to allow both men and women to more comfortably balance the demands of family and work. Working against this shift is the extremely competitive nature of coaches and administrators that is so pervasive in the athletic culture. Therefore, ways in which to lessen the demands of recruiting, practice, and travel must continue to be explored. It would be self-defeating if college athletics developed to a point where to be successful would require a choice between family and profession.

Further, additional changes designed to keep women in the field must be implemented. Specifically, salary benefits and job descriptions for women must be comparable to those of men. For example, many women coaches also are assigned administrative duties, whereas men coaches in the same sport are not. The task of attracting competent women into the field is much more difficult if they are treated as second-class citizens in the areas of salary benefits and job descriptions.

3. *Increased Professional Development Opportunities.* While the number of professional development opportunities for women has been increasing, largely through the efforts of the National Association for College Women's Athletic Administrators (NACWAA), these opportunities must be expanded further. Correspondingly, institutions must provide support in the form of time and resources to allow women to take advantage of those opportunities. In many cases, women are unable to attend professional development workshops and programs because the athletic department has not provided for them in the budget. Further, women must become more aggressive in taking advantage of such

opportunities when they present themselves, not only in the form of NACWAA programs, but also those professional development opportunities involving men. Women must become more aggressive in taking advantage of informal networking functions, programs, and events (e.g., golf events, cocktail parties, etc.). While being in a male-dominated field presents challenges in tapping into "the network," those challenges are not insurmountable.

4. *More Access to Decision-Making Processes.* Finally, women must be provided more opportunities to "be at the table" with men in the decision-making processes of sports organizations and athletic departments. For example, the six top leadership positions in the new NCAA governance structure are occupied by men. Simply put, men need to be more open to new ideas and must be willing to "make room" for those who might see sports a bit differently from them. And, of course, once seated at those tables, women must have the courage to speak up.

THE FEMINIZATION OF ATHLETIC DEPARTMENTS

How might athletic programs be affected by a significant increase of women in key administrative and coaching positions? In other words, what is the payoff for implementing suggestions such as those just mentioned? To envision such a scenario, it is best to turn to corporate America, where the effects of increased women in the workplace are starting to be felt. While men still hold most of the management positions, women are making significant inroads into the corporate decision-making structure. As might be expected, organizational behavior and management researchers are examining those effects. The result is a growing body of theory and research indicating that female leaders influence the workplace differently than men (Smith & Smits, 1994). As a result, "a new model of leadership, one that emphasizes persuasion over power, cooperation over competition, collectivism over individualism, and inclusion over exclusion is in ascendence" (Lee, 1994, p. 26). Aburdene and Naisbitt (1992) concur:

> Primitive descriptions of the "manager of the future" uncannily match those of female leadership. Consultants tried to teach male managers to relinquish the command-and-control mode. For women, it was different: it just came naturally. . . . Management guru Peter Drucker vows that Frances Hesselbein, former director of the Girl Scouts and a foremost example of this new leadership, "could manage any company in America." Tom Peters, author of

In Search of Excellence, tells men, "who wish to stay employed" to study women's ways of leadership (pp. 88–89).

Sally Helgesen, author of several books about women's management styles, takes the argument a step further, stating: "Increasingly, motherhood is being recognized as an excellent school for managers, demanding many of the same skills: organization, pacing, the balancing of conflicting claims, teaching, guiding, leading, monitoring, handling disturbances, imparting information" (Helgesen as cited in Aburdene & Naisbitt, 1992, p. 94).

Authors Connie Glaser and Barbara Steinberg Smalley further identify the differences between male and female leadership styles in *Swim with the Dolphins: How Women Can Succeed in Corporate America on Their Own Terms* (1995). They characterize male managers as generally using the "shark" model of leadership. "Sharks are stern taskmasters who relish power. Their approach is strictly top-down, leaving no doubt whatsoever about who's in charge. They bark orders to their subordinates, expecting obedience and loyalty in return . . . their concerns are with the bottom line, not with people" (p. 8). The authors suggest that women are more likely to employ a leadership style more representative of a "dolphin."

> In contrast to the sharks, dolphins prefer operating in webs rather than hierarchies. They seek respect (rather than obedience) from subordinates and recognize that loyalty cannot be demanded; it must be earned. Like the sharks, dolphins are concerned with the bottom line, but they are equally focused on the people who work for them. . . . . Dolphins are comfortable with power, but rarely abuse it. They view themselves as "leaders" rather than "bosses." (p. 9)

According to Glaser and Smalley (1995), "with their tough but caring ways, dolphins are not only revitalizing the workforce, they are changing the way America's companies do business. . . . At last, women can acknowledge the fact that we *are* different, because different is good" (pp. 10–11).

If women's leadership styles are indeed different from men's, how can this difference affect the management of athletic programs?

For example, women tend to be more nurturing in their approach to people and relationships, a trait that has obvious benefits for the young people in our programs. Further, women's leadership style is more likely to be collegial (leadership through consensus) than autocratic. In an era when input from student-athletes should become increasingly important, such a leadership style would suggest a more open, collaborative, and inclusive environment in which student-athletes would be provided increasing opportunities to become a part of the decision-making process. Such an approach also might address some of the concerns of Black student-athletes, coaches, and administrators who feel disenfranchised in a system that they were so instrumental in building and maintaining.

Organizational research also indicates that the way in which men and women wield leadership influence also differs. Men tend to influence through exercise of their positional power, while women are more likely to influence through persuasion and interpersonal networking. This difference could have a significant influence on the general philosophy of athletic departments as it relates to the teaching component of higher education's mission. Such an approach suggests a greater emphasis on discussion, dialogue, and persuasion, clearly an approach that more closely parallels a teaching, rather than a dictatorial, style of interpersonal interaction, and certainly an approach that is more appropriate for programs sponsored by an academic institution. With increasing concern that coaches and athletic administrators have forsaken their primary roles as teachers and educators, such a change may serve to help them reconnect with their teaching responsibilities.

Women's leadership styles also place greater emphasis on cooperation and fair play as opposed to the prevailing notion of leadership as a competitive, win-at-all-costs proposition. The potential positive effect of women's leadership in this area is significant. Educational leaders must begin to address the win-at-all-costs attitude that permeates athletic programs at the high school, college, and even youth levels. Could it be that with more women in positions of influence in athletics, we could begin to address in earnest the negative effects that such an attitude has on our educational system? While winning will always be important, and women want to win as much as men, women "understand that winning and losing are not the black-and-white dichotomy they seem to be" (Nelson, 1998, p. 10). Women's apparent greater sensitivity to "fair play" presents interesting opportunities as sports leaders throughout the nation struggle to address what appears to be a decline in sportsmanship and ethical behavior in our coaches and athletes.

In sum, there is growing public concern regarding the role of athletics within our educational system. Charges of exploitation of student-athletes, alienation from the academic community, an excessive emphasis on outcomes (winning) as opposed to participation, and a general decline in ethical standards and sportsmanship are concerns of increasing significance. By all indications, women may possess some of the much-needed leadership skills and attitudes to help the athletic community address these issues.

SEEKING BALANCE

There is more at stake in the issue of women's "equality of opportunity" than simply numbers. Such change is important because there are significant programmatic and philosophical benefits that unquestionably will accrue as a result of such change.

The issue is balance. If anyone would understand the benefits that balance can bring to an organization, it would be leaders in the field of athletics. Any coach or athletic director knows that a basketball team with 5 one-dimensional players will likely lose more than it wins. That is why coaches try to round out their teams with players who have a diverse array of skills. To be successful, a team must be balanced with scorers, rebounders, ballhandlers, shooters, and one or two defensive "stoppers." It is only by maximizing the strengths and minimizing the weaknesses of each player, only by blending their diverse talents, that a group of individuals will mesh into a highly effective team.

Similarly, it is only through a diverse leadership group that athletics will maximize its potential to contribute to the goals and mission of our nation's colleges and schools. Such a model would celebrate the unique strengths of both men and women. Despite what some may think, calls for gender equity do not mean the downfall of sport as we know it. It does not mean that men must be replaced as administrators and coaches. Rather, it means that athletics will be far better off, far stronger and a much more viable component of the educational system, if we encourage feminine styles of leadership to balance the existing masculine styles. Just like our basketball team, men and women have got to "share the rock" if we expect athletics to come out a winner.

REFERENCES

Aburdene, P., & Naisbitt, J. (1992). *Megatrends for women*. New York: Villard Books.

Acosta, V. R., & Carpenter, L. J. (1996). *Women in intercollegiate sport: A longitudinal study, 1977–1996*. Brooklyn, NY: Brooklyn College, Department of Physical Education.

Coakley, J. J. (1998). *Sport and society, issues and controversies*. New York: Mosby-Year Books.

Collegiate Commissioners Association. (1997). *1997–98 Directory*. Bethlehem, PA: Collegiate Commissioners Association.

Corbin, C., & Pangrazi, B. (1997, September). Youth sports in America: An overview. *President's Council on Physical Fitness and Sports Research Digest* (Series 2:No. 11). Washington, DC: U.S. Government Printing Office.

Davenport, J. (1996, May/June). Breaking into the rights: Women on the IOC. *Journal of Physical Education, Recreation, and Dance*, pp. 26–30.

Equal Employment Opportunity Commission. (1997). *Enforcement guidance on sex discrimination in the compensation of sports coaches in educational institutions.* Washington, DC: Author.

Glaser, C., & Smalley, B. S. (1995). *Swim with the dolphins: How women can succeed in corporate America on their own terms.* New York: Warner Books.

Lee, C. (1994, November). The feminization of management. *Training, 31*(11), 25–31.

National Collegiate Athletic Association. (1997). *NCAA gender equity study summary of results.* Overland Park, KS: Author.

Nelson, M. B. (1998). *Embracing victory: Life lessons in competition and compassion.* New York: Morrow.

Smith, P. L., & Smits, S. J. (1994, February). The feminization of leadership? *Training & Development*, pp. 43–46.

U.S. Office of Civil Rights. Statement of findings presented in a March 1, 1995 letter to Wichita State University President Eugene H. Hughes (Docket No. 07932071).

Wenninger, M. D. (1997, November). New women A.D.s at Tennessee, W. Michigan. *Women in Higher Education, 6*(11), 4.

Wichita State University. (1995, June). *Plan for corrective action.* Submitted to the Department of Education, U.S. Office of Civil Rights.

PART IV

Athletics and Education:
A Good Investment?

THE CLAIM THAT athletics participation plays a critical role in the educational process has been a widely held assumption in the United States. As proof of the intensity of this belief, one needs only to consider the tremendous amount of money, time, and emotion invested in youth sports leagues, high school teams, and college programs nationwide. As discussed in previous chapters, it is arguable whether many of the alleged educational benefits of sports programs—principles on which this investment is justified—are, in fact, real.

Bob Bigelow raised serious concerns regarding the motives and purposes of youth programs. Sharon Stoll and Jennifer Beller presented research that calls into question the claim that athletics participation builds positive character traits. Michael Clark and Andrew Kreutzer noted that many of today's coaches and athletic administrators are not prepared to fulfill their educational responsibilities. Darren Bilberry maintained that the claim that athletics provides thousands of Blacks with a meaningful educational opportunity is a myth. These and other questions raised throughout this book are significant because they challenge specific elements of the fundamental notion that athletics has a positive influence on the educational process, that it contributes in very direct and meaningful ways to our country's educational enterprise.

Achieving long-lasting and meaningful change, however, requires attention to not only the specific elements that make up the whole, but also the general tenets upon which the system is built. To capture the entire picture of sport's role in our nation's educational landscape, we must consider both the specific and the general, the practical as well as the philosophical. To that end, Part 4 takes on a decidedly more philosophical tone, placing the specific concerns and issues raised by the previous authors in a broader context. For example, given the sum total of the concerns raised in the previous chapters, should athletics even be part of our educational system? Is it the extracurricular activity best suited to produce worthwhile educational results? What is its cumulative effect on our nation's attitudes regarding education, health and fitness, and race and gender? In this concluding part, we will explore the issue of sport and education from this broader and more philosophical perspective.

In "Athletics and the Higher Education Marketplace," Cynthia Patterson asserts that the changing higher education marketplace leaves no choice but to "outsource" major college athletics as an auxiliary enterprise, eliminating any direct ties to the academic process. She writes that educational leaders have been unable to reform athletics, not due to a lack of resolve, but because in responding to a rapidly changing higher education marketplace, they have come to embrace the very market-driven philosophies and practices long employed by athletic departments. Revenue enhancement, product promotion, and cost control have become as much a part of decision making in the halls of academe as they have been in the athletic department. The author argues that athletic reform may be the most critical issue facing American higher education because it offers such a clear choice between mission and marketing, business and education, and expediency over institutional purpose, all challenges that higher education itself must confront as it struggles to maintain institutional integrity in the face of an increasingly competitive marketplace.

If the previous contributors are correct in their assessment that athletics does not generate as positive an educational benefit as previously thought, how should we respond as a society? As we struggle to prepare our workforce to compete successfully in the global, information-based economy of the twenty-first century, while at the same time educational dollars are becoming more scarce, should we continue to invest in expensive programs that reap only marginal educational benefits? For example, perhaps the resources currently invested in athletics would result in greater educational return if spent on music programs. While some may consider such an idea blasphemous, it is not, if, as articulated by the editor in Chapter 11, such programs are compared using educational benefits and outcomes as the standard.

In Chapter 12, Robert McCabe, writes that despite its immense popularity with millions of Americans, extremely high visibility in mainstream media, enormous financial impact, and central role in our national identity, sport contributes very little of substance to our culture. According to McCabe, mega-commercialized sport has lost its meaning in the American experience, having become a negative influence that is tearing at the fabric of our society. He argues that the folly of our current devotion to the "spectacle of sport" must be challenged. To that end, he calls for the "depopularization" of sport as mass entertainment and a re-engagement with sports participation as a way to add value to our lives on a daily basis.

In the final chapter, Bill Curry places the discussion regarding sport's role in the educational process in a broader perspective by drawing upon the lessons of history. Curry suggests that the issues we face today—misplaced values, corruption, and a gross overemphasis on athletics—are identical to those faced by the ancient Greeks. That being the case, he proposes that we simply accept the premise that a certain societal obsession with sport is inevitable, that it is a fact of the human condition. Curry, a two-time Super Bowl champion and former football coach at Georgia Tech and the Universities of Alabama and Kentucky, follows with a thoughtful reflection of a career spent in athletics. He passionately describes athletics' tremendous power and potential for both good and bad. Curry is correct when he implies that there are no easy answers to the questions raised in this book. His vivid analysis of the many contradictions surrounding our society's embrace of athletics perhaps best describes the essence of the debate on the role of athletics in the educational process.

10

Athletics and the Higher Education Marketplace

Cynthia M. Patterson

At the 1997 national meeting of the American Council on Education (ACE), more than 1,300 presidents and other senior administrators representing over 900 college and universities gathered to discuss major issues confronting higher education. Presentations from President Bill Clinton, Senate Majority Leader Trent Lott, and a host of national leaders in government, education, and industry underscored the power, authority, and influence of the gathered multitude. In a program containing more than 30 sessions, only one session focused on intercollegiate athletics.

In stark contrast to the relative insignificance of intercollegiate athletics to the membership of the ACE, one month later millions of Americans participated in the annual ritual of "March Madness." As millions of dollars rolled into the coffers of the NCAA and its member institutions, the fact that the overwhelming majority of the players themselves would never graduate from college seemed as insignificant to the sponsors, fans, and participants in the NCAA Men's Basketball Championship as the session on restructuring the NCAA had been to the leadership of higher education.

As I sat among the 15 or so individuals (most of whom had to be recruited into the ACE session to create an audience) listening to the panel discuss the restructuring of the NCAA, I wondered why the problems of intercollegiate athletics no longer commanded urgent calls for reform from within either the halls of academe or the court of public opinion.

Today, as in the past, many continue to assume that the profound contradictions between the goals and values of higher education and the commercialization and overt hypocrisy of major college athletics have become so entrenched that meaningful and lasting reform is no longer possible. Given the economic and cultural power of college sports within

American society, it is easy to understand why urgent calls for systemic change to eliminate the abuses of intercollegiate athletics in the 1980s resulted in retreat rather than reform. As the *Kansas City Star's* 1997 special report, "Money Games! Inside the NCAA," clearly demonstrated, the business of college sports is booming. Operating with an annual budget of $270 million, the NCAA oversees a multimillion dollar sports cartel whose 100-plus Division I-A schools generate average annual revenues of $4 million per school (McGraw, Rock, & Dillon, 1997).

According to this perspective, many presidents, administrators, and faculty view college sports as a necessary, if often problematic, component of university life. Whether a fan or critic, many college officials appear to have made an uneasy peace with intercollegiate athletics, accepting it as an unnatural intruder protected by forces beyond institutional control.

Thus, it has become widely accepted that big-time college sports and education operate in two distinct and virtually separate worlds. Contrary to prevailing beliefs, however, the gaps between big-time college sports and the norms and values of both higher education and the public are not as vast as reformers assumed. Today, college sports have more in common with both American society and the world of higher education than anyone has dared to acknowledge. Ironically, as the public's willingness to tolerate the excesses of college sports is becoming increasingly fragile, subtle changes within higher education itself have fostered a strange, new climate of both support and commitment to the athletic status quo. It is this change and its effect on the future of American higher education that will be the focus of this chapter.

FAILED REFORM

The publication of the Knight Foundation Commission on Intercollegiate Athletics report, *Keeping Faith with the Student-Athlete: A New Model for Intercollegiate Athletics,* in March 1991, led many to believe that the day of reckoning for college sports had finally arrived. After 18 months of study, the $2 million, 47-page report marked the culmination of a decade-long movement to remedy the ills plaguing big-time sports. Calling on presidents and the leadership of higher education to reassert control over college athletics, the Knight Commission (1991) identified "the great reversal of ends and means" as the root of the problem that had placed "sports as education" on the edge of disaster.

> Increasingly, the team, the game, the season and "the program"—all intended as expressions of the university's larger purposes—gain ascendancy

over the ends that created and nurtured them. Non-revenue sports receive little attention, and women's programs take a back seat. As the educational context for collegiate competition is pushed aside, what remains is, too often, a self-justifying enterprise whose connection with learning is tainted by commercialism and incipient cynicism. (p. 4)

Following the path of every other major attempt to reform athletics since the founding of the NCAA in 1906, the efforts of the Knight Commission and the athletic reform movement it inspired, failed. Describing its recommendations as little more than "symbolic reform," *Washington Post* columnist Jonathan Yardley (1991) summed up the place of college sports within higher education as follows:

The Knight Commission recognizes that big-time intercollegiate sport is now so indigenous to American business and culture that its fundamental character can never change: the most we can hope for is to clean it up a bit, and that's what the Knight Commission proposes to do. (p. B-1)

The power of the NCAA and major athletic programs to resist and even co-opt every significant attack and corresponding call for change is truly one of the most disturbing victories recorded in the history of higher education. Citing the report as a testimonial to "accommodation and compromise," Yardley (1991) concluded that the failure of the Commission and of efforts at radical reform lies squarely with the lack of bold, courageous, and enlightened leadership within higher education.

But it wasn't simply resistance within the college athletic establishment that thwarted meaningful reform. By the time the Knight Commission released its report, the institutional and societal preconditions for systemic reform were already disappearing from within the academy. Presidents and other educational leaders failed to reform abuses in athletics not because of a loss of nerve or ignorance about the problem, but, rather because they were participants in the transformation of colleges and universities from guardians of academic integrity, ethical conduct, and institutional mission to market-driven businesses as obsessed with image, self-promotion, and "the product" as any athletic enterprise. As a result of this shift, it has become increasingly difficult, if not impossible, to tell the difference between the goals and values of higher education and those of college sports.

HIGHER EDUCATION'S NEW MARKETPLACE

At one time, the market-driven, profit-making goals and win-at-all-costs values of Division I athletics had been a clear exception to the mission and purpose of colleges and universities. But as a result of today's rapidly changing higher education marketplace, athletics and higher education have found a common ground in values and practices that assert the priorities of merely "good business."

In unprecedented ways, the 1990s ushered in an era of intense public scrutiny and self-examination within higher education. Confronting changing demographics that intensified competition for students, reductions in governmental financial support, and a growing body of criticism questioning the effectiveness of every aspect of institutional life, colleges and universities struggled to adapt and respond to a rapidly changing environment. As debates within the academy focused on curriculum reform, rediscovering the importance of teaching and learning, and assessing quality outcomes, public perceptions of higher education became increasingly critical. As economic hard times forced colleges and universities to adopt new strategies and behaviors, tensions between faithful commitment to mission and fiscal realities intensified. For inherently risk-adverse institutions like colleges and universities, the challenge of defining, creating, and implementing widespread change created a fertile climate for both innovation and self-preservation.

As institutional decision making was redefined in terms of revenue enhancement and responses to the demands of the marketplace, the norms and values of higher education shifted away from mission and purpose. Educational priorities were no longer immune from the vicissitudes of the marketplace. Consequently, colleges and universities found themselves struggling to find ways to respond to the realities of the marketplace without destroying the values, ideals, and purposes that remained essential to both their missions as educational institutions and their responsibilities as democratic institutions. For higher education leaders, the lines of distinction between "good business" and "good education" were becoming increasingly blurred.

Thus, as the greatest rivalry in college sports moved from the playing fields of Harvard and Yale to the marketing departments of Nike and Reebok, competition between colleges and universities shifted from an emphasis on academic programs and educational quality to "marketing strategies," "image building," revenue enhancement, and cost control. Recruiting students through special promotions, videos, slick marketing campaigns, and financial inducements, once the exclusive expertise of Division I athletics, defines virtually all aspects of the new industry of "enrollment management." Improving their institution's rankings in the *Princeton Review* or the best-selling *U.S. News and World Report's College Guide* is now as important to most college and university presidents as the weekly top 25 polls are to coaches. Privatization of services, licensing of logos and products, and corporate sponsorship are becoming as commonplace within the ivory tower as within the world of major college sports.

So, at the very time that critics of college sports were condemning the moral and educational bankruptcy of big-time athletics, college and university officials were sounding more and more like Nike executives and corporate managers than like educators and scholars. As higher education leaders began to confront the demands of the marketplace, their ability and willingness to approach college sports with a critical eye and independent judgment decreased. The reform movement in college athletics, therefore, lost momentum at precisely the same time because colleges and universities adopted many of the practices, principles, values, and rationalizations found within athletics.

For example, the athletic scholarship, once the only form of non-academic merit aid in higher education, competes with "yield scholarships" and "tuition discounts" for financial aid dollars. Competition for students fuels an unprecedented expansion in extracurricular services, recreational facilities, and other nonacademic enterprises that reflect the excesses of athletic programs in a new, less critical, and academic light.

The problem here is not simply that colleges and universities must compete successfully in a highly competitive marketplace, or that the emergence of marketing, commercialization, and issues of price, cost, and financial management are inherently destructive to institutional mission and purpose. The problem is that sports and education are both on the edge of becoming collaborators in the triumph of images over ideas and in the ascendancy of the marketplace over the goals and values of education in a democratic society.

In a 1997 edition of *The Educational Record*, the President of the ACE, Stanley Ikenberry, commenting on the growing commercialization of colleges and universities, offered these words of caution:

> The lines between healthy competition and commercialization, between self-reliance and opportunism, between creativity and exploitation, between good taste and hucksterism, and between opportunity and compromising purpose are almost never clear. . . . What happens, however, when the values of academic life appear to be threatened or compromised and when an institution—be it through tuition pricing policy, the exploitation of intellectual property rights or the conduct of its athletics program—appears more committed to its own financial well-being than to the society it serves? (p. 7)

In other words, in the life of the university, athletics, or otherwise, does the "price" or "cost" of surviving take precedence over institutional purpose, integrity, and effectiveness?

CONFRONTING TRUTHS

To create a new impetus for reform in college sports, we must be willing to evaluate the strengths and weaknesses of the current system with both clarity and critical detachment. Looking at athletics from this perspective means looking at ourselves as participants, rather than bystanders, in the perpetuation of self-justifying and self-serving canons of thought and action that undermine both education and sports.

The first truth we need to embrace is that big-time college athletics is an entertainment industry, not an educational endeavor. As a former colleague of mine often said, "We do not compare SAT scores on the 50-yard line." The very nature of contemporary professional and college sports stands independent of education. The skills, abilities, and qualities of athletic success are not dependent on academic skills or abilities.

Despite the public's awareness of the abuses within big-time college sports, the simple fact remains that we have accepted the role of intercollegiate athletics as entertainment. We love sports. Our love affair with sports has encouraged us to abandon the romantic notion that professional and semiprofessional college athletics should be anything more than pure entertainment. The rise of the professional athlete as entertainer and superstar reveals the depth of our cultural need to be entertained and our willingness to accept the reality of sports as mass entertainment.

A second and related truth is that it is virtually impossible for most Americans to view athletes as victims. Athletes do not make empathetic victims because we view them as privileged elite. They possess what almost every American wishes he or she had—a special talent that brings the individual both adulation and huge financial rewards. Multimillion dollar contracts and endorsement deals, access to "the good life," and the opportunity to be a celebrity and a hero bestow upon athletes both cultural admiration and envy. At a time when most Americans struggle to balance the demands of work and family, worry about the stagnation in family incomes, and feel increasingly isolated and disillusioned about both institutions and leaders, athletes represent the last of a dying breed—the self-made individual who succeeds or fails on his or her own. It is almost un-American to shift our ideological gears enough to view athletes as victims of any system or form of exploitation. The power of the myth of individualism, infused with the cult of celebrity, is far too entrenched in the fantasy lives of most individuals for anyone to see athletes as anything but a fortunate elite whose flaws, failures, and misfortunes are almost always self-inflicted.

Given these values and attitudes, it is easy to explain why we have accepted the rationalizations of the sports establishment for the negative and often exploitative consequences of big-time college sports for student-athletes. If the student-athlete fails to graduate, the institution did not fail, the athlete did. The misbehavior of athletes on and off the field reflects dysfunctional families or declining values throughout society. In case after case, the athletic system and those who run it are rarely held accountable.

Our collective failure to acknowledge these realities has placed coaches, administrators, athletes, and educators in the untenable position of trying to rationalize and defend a system of college sports that ultimately undermines the best interests of all. As currently constructed, major college sports produce more losers than winners. The student-athletes are the biggest losers. It is clear that colleges and universities are willing to compromise academic standards to achieve athletic success, but these compromises have become the basis for a self-justifying set of half-truths that now serve as a valid explanation for the compromises themselves.

For example, the most common defense of preferential admissions policies for athletes, special academic support programs, and low graduation rates in Division I men's football and basketball is that athletes often come from disadvantaged backgrounds and/or have special needs that demand special treatment. But this position is a statement of the problem rather than a testimonial to the effectiveness of colleges and universities in serving the educational needs of all student-athletes. If college sports conformed to academic standards, then special treatment and special services for athletes would be unnecessary. In fact, if children playing sports in junior high and high school knew that admission to college depended more on their academic preparation than on their athletic talent, then studying would be more important than practicing.

Even though the odds of any high school athlete playing professional sports are 10,000 to 1, 66% of all African-American males between the ages of 13 and 18 believe they can earn a living as a professional athlete (Simons, 1997). At Division I institutions, African-Americans constitute just 6.6% of total undergraduate enrollment, yet they make up 46% and 60% of the men's football and basketball programs, respectively (Naughton, 1997). From the press releases of the NCAA to the promotional speeches of coaches and college officials, the myth of athletics as a means of social mobility and opportunity remains virtually unchallenged. Nike ads implore children to "Just Do It," and colleges and universities, for their part, refuse to accept responsibility for creating expectations among children and their parents that athletics more than academics holds the key to collegiate and professional success.

CHOOSING HONESTLY

The fact that higher education now shares a common set of values, practices, and priorities with college sports has heightened, rather than reduced, the need for reform in athletics. Even though the values of the marketplace have compromised the ability of many institutions to strike a balance between business and education, the intensity of the debates within higher education reveals that there are still choices available. The academy can and must reflect critically on the tortured logic and misplaced priorities within college sports to refocus its own energies on reasserting the values of academic life and providing legitimate alternatives to "survival at all costs."

Individuals who care about education will recognize that preserving specific institutions or specific types of activities within higher education is fraught with danger. For many colleges and universities, institutional survival itself may be a false expectation! Shattering the myth that the demand for every service, program, and even specific institution itself, is necessary and will be painful. The failure to accept this pain with honesty, creativity, and integrity will endanger the university even further.

Perhaps the greatest danger facing higher education today is that the similarities between college sports and the academy will continue to expand. While the choices required to avert a disaster within the academic world are exceedingly complex, the intense concern, discussion, and conflict within and beyond the academic community offer genuine hope for new leadership and action. On the other hand, the choices regarding the role of college sports as education are not as difficult. In fact, if we cannot radically redefine the role of college sports, we will run the risk of losing the battle to reinvent and preserve higher education itself, for we will have demonstrated an inability to understand the differences between mission and marketing.

What would happen if we told the truth and acted on it? What would happen if we redefined college sports in ways that acknowledged the role of elite athletic programs as auxiliary services for colleges and universities and as training grounds for professional sports? For the limited number of big-time programs that compete at the highest levels and are financially self-supporting, their true role would be as an "outsourced," auxiliary enterprise with the sole purpose of supporting the institution through revenue and public relations. Coaches and athletes would contribute their services as salaried employees without any direct ties to the educational process.

What if we returned all other, "nonprofessional" athletic programs to their proper place within the educational institution? Athletic scholarships would disappear as would all the other special arrangements that undermine the dignity, integrity, and purpose of both education and sports. Such a change would ensure that college athletics would no longer be "on the edge," but rather either returned to its rightful place within the mainstream educational community as a co-curricular activity or removed from it altogether. No more contradictions. No more lies. No more self-perpetuating myths. Most important, it would represent a clear choice between the images of the marketplace and the values of education.

As higher education re-examines its purposes, practices, values, and mission, the failure of athletics presents an urgent opportunity for genuine reform to triumph over expediency. Such attempts will see more questioning of the increasingly dangerous tendency to proclaim that survival is an excuse for accepting compromises that ultimately betray institutional integrity. The athletic world offers a clear model of what is happening as the goals and values of educational institutions become subservient to those of the marketplace. For leaders in higher education today, the battleground for saving the heart and soul of higher education is no longer limited to curbing the excesses of renegade athletic programs. As Pogo observed, "We have seen the enemy, and it is us."

ACKNOWLEDGMENT

The author is grateful to Joe Wilson for his assistance with this chapter.

REFERENCES

Ikenberry, S. O. (1997, Winter). The entrepreneurial campus: A time for innovation (and caution). *The Educational Record*, pp. 7–8.

Knight Foundation Commission on Intercollegiate Athletics. (1991). *Keeping faith with the student-athlete: A new model for intercollegiate athletics.* Charlotte, NC: Knight Foundation.

McGraw, M., Rock, S., & Dillon, K. (1997, October 5–11). Money games! Inside the NCAA. *Kansas City Star.*

Naughton, J. (1997, July 25). Athletes lack grades and test scores of other students. *The Chronicle of Higher Education*, p. A-43.

Simons, J. (1997, March 24). Improbable dreams. *U.S. News and World Report*, pp. 46–52.

Yardley, J. (1991, March 25). Crying foul over the Knight report. *Washington Post*, p. B-1.

11

Want Value for Education Dollars? Try Music!

John R. Gerdy

As outlined in the Introduction, it was the influence and support of the great industrialists of the early twentieth century that paved the way for the widespread development of youth sports programs and the incorporation of athletic programs into America's educational system. Athletics not only promoted good health, but also instilled in participants the types of character traits that made successful and productive factory workers, socialized the growing number of immigrants into the "American" way of life, and aided in national military preparedness. Business leaders of the day saw in organized athletics an activity that could contribute positively to the nation's educational goals while meeting the manpower needs of their growing industrial empires. By all indications, sport was successful in meeting these purposes.

That was almost a century ago. From the peach basket and leather football helmet to the luxury box and multibillion dollar television contract, the growth and commercialization of sport are something that the educational leaders and industrialists of the past could never have fathomed. How have these changes affected sports programs' ability to contribute to meeting our nation's educational purposes? Do those cultural, educational, and economic objectives that seemed so relevant almost 100 years ago, remain so today? If so, are modern-day sports programs meeting those objectives? Given such change in our cultural, educational, and economic landscape, these are questions that responsible educators, parents, and taxpayers can not afford to ignore.

ARE WE MEETING OUR GOALS?

While the health benefits that accrue to athletes are well documented, they remain a vague afterthought to coaches and athletic administrators.

As suggested by Bob Bigelow and Bob McCabe, our sports programs are elitist and exclusionary, neither designed nor conducted with the health benefits of participants in mind. If we were interested in deriving the greatest health return on dollars spent on athletics, more resources would be spent on broad-based, participatory, intramural, club, and physical education programs than on the current programs designed to cater to a small population of elite athletes. If community and education leaders were committed to using athletic participation as a tool to improve public health, school systems would be strengthening, rather than weakening, physical education requirements and appropriating increasingly scarce public education dollars to these programs rather than to the football or basketball teams. At the college level, athletic programs with budgets in excess of $25 million that provide opportunities for less than 5% of the student body simply would not exist. The health benefits associated with participation in a competitive athletic program can easily be achieved, at a far lesser expense, by participating in recreational activities ranging from intramurals, to physical education classes, to individual sports activities such as jogging or swimming.

Is the link between sports and military preparedness a valid justification for our continued heavy investment in sports? The United States has won the Cold War. Military service is now voluntary. Trends in military preparedness have resulted in a downsizing of troops in favor of increased investment in military technology and weaponry. These factors suggest that sports' role in military preparedness may be outdated as the skills necessary to perform successfully in the high-tech military of the future are just as likely to be learned in the classroom and computer lab as on the playing fields.

Finally, as explained by Derrick Gragg and Darren Bilberry in Chapters 7 and 8, respectively, the connection between sports participation and upward mobility is a cruel illusion, serving to lure far too many children, particularly inner-city Blacks, further and further away from the classroom.

CHANGING EDUCATIONAL PRIORITIES IN THE INFORMATION AGE

Perhaps the most critical aspect of the discussion regarding our nation's changing sports and educational landscape, and the focus of this chapter, relates to the role of athletic participation in developing the skills necessary to succeed in the workplace. Business leaders of today have been expressing increasing concern regarding the inability of our educational system to develop in the future workforce, the educational skills needed to keep American companies competitive in a high-tech, information-based, global economy. A common complaint is that too much emphasis, in terms of not only dollars but, more important, time and effort, is being placed on maintaining highly competitive athletic programs, often at the expense of educational programs in music, math, art, or the sciences.

Texas industrialist H. Ross Perot's involvement in an educational reform effort in that state provides an excellent example of athletics' negative effect on educational priorities and outcomes. One element of Texas's reform packet required students involved in extracurricular activities to earn at least a C in all of their courses. This aspect of the reform initiative received the most attention as it would apply to student-athletes. Apparently, many Texans were interested in educational reform provided it did not affect the quality of their high school athletic programs. This is hardly a recipe conducive to preparing our future workforce to compete successfully in the information age.

The characteristics organized sport instills in participants—punctuality, unquestioned respect for authority, hard work, teamwork, and so on—were desirable job characteristics for the factory worker of the industrial age. Factory owners of that time did not want their line workers to be great thinkers, preferring that they passively accept the status quo. "The leaders of American industry felt that their workers needed to be loyal and punctual, but not necessarily good academically" (Miracle & Rees, 1994, p. 178).

Do the workforce skills that were valued during the industrial revolution serve our country's economic interests as we enter into the twenty-first century? While the ability to work in a team environment, punctuality, hard work, and discipline are all desirable worker traits, preparing our country's workforce to compete successfully in the information-based, service economy of the new millennium requires much more—specifically, the ability to reason, think creatively, manage large amounts of information, and critically assess data, and improved math, verbal, and communication skills. The information age requires strong minds developed in the classrooms more than strong bodies developed on the playing fields. What Andrew Carnegie considered to be good worker skills for purposes of advancing America's economic interests in 1900 may not be considered adequate by today's business leaders, such as Perot or Microsoft's Bill Gates, to advance America's economic interests in 2000 and beyond.

If this is so, what does it mean for our nation's youth, high school, and college athletic programs? What effect will our continued public investment in what may very well be outdated "educational" programs have on our future economic competitiveness? Can we as taxpayers afford to continue to appropriate precious "educational" resources for programs that promote and develop skills better suited to serving the aging factories of the Rust Belt than the emerging high-tech enterprises of Silicon Valley?

Beyond the issue of worker preparedness lies a much more compelling question. Could it be that the overemphasis placed on athletics in our educational system actually has a negative effect on academic achievement and educational priorities?

Wayne Flynt, Distinguished University Professor at Auburn University, speaks often about misplaced educational priorities. During an April 25, 1990 speech, Flynt discussed the release of a study indicating that four of Birmingham, Alabama's 10 high schools had no students who scored at or above the national average in reading, math, language, and science between 1985 and 1987 and, of the six remaining high schools, none had more than 17% of their students scoring at or above the national average. He noted that not only was Birmingham's system well above the average for the state, but that "of nearly 400 high schools in Alabama, about 370 field football teams. But only 286 offered a foreign language course in 1988 and fewer than 100 offered full fledged computer courses."

Flynt (1994) did not limit his concern regarding the adverse effect of Alabama's overemphasis on sports on educational priorities to the high school level.

> At a more profound level the success of Alabama athletics left a mixed legacy. The football success of two otherwise undistinguishable state universities (Auburn and Alabama) during the 1950's and 1960's provided an athletic equivalent to Governor Wallace's contempt for "pointy-headed intellectuals" and "cerebral wimps." This overemphasis on football made it harder to recruit talented faculty or academically gifted students, many of whom left the state for schools with better-equipped laboratories and more challenging curricula even if their football programs struggled to break even. (p. 586)

While the value of competitive athletic programs can be debated, that the world has changed dramatically since the incorporation of such programs into our educational system, can not. As a result, our nation's educational system is being scrutinized as never before. In response, community and educational leaders are struggling to address the multitude of issues involved in reassessing educational priorities and preparing our populace to meet the workplace challenges of the coming millennium. As a significant and highly visible component of that educational system, our heavy investment in athletics also must be scrutinized.

IS THERE A BETTER INVESTMENT?

Is athletics the extracurricular activity best suited to prepare our children and our country to compete successfully in the global marketplace of the future? Arguably not. Despite claims from the athletic establishment to the contrary, there is little to suggest that participation in athletics develops the intellectual skills necessary to excel in the information age. "The evidence shows that being an athlete does not improve one's chances of being a good student and that sport does not make poor students good students or good students even better" (Miracle & Rees, 1994, p. 178).

Even Theodore Roosevelt, one of our country's most enthusiastic promoters of sport, recognized its limitations as a vehicle to prepare young people to succeed in the workforce. In *The American Boy* he stated: "We can not expect the best work from soldiers who have carried to an unhealthy extreme the sports and pastimes which would be healthy if indulged in with moderation, and have neglected to learn as they should the business of their profession" (as cited in Mrozek, 1983, p. 35). Mrozek (1983) points out:

> [The] distinction he [Roosevelt] made was a crucial one—sport gave one qualities of character and not transferrable skills, further undermining the notion of easily equating sport with other activities. The superiority of sport over war in the shaping of character lay in the fact that it was less likely to kill the participants; but sport had no advantage in preparing one for the practical aspects of war, business or politics, and Roosevelt knew it. (p. 35)

What then would be a more prudent investment of educational resources? Music.

"Music programs?" critics will ask. "Playing the flute won't build character like getting knocked down on the football field. And nothing teaches teamwork better than sports."

To think that one can develop characteristics such as perseverance, teamwork, communication skills, and discipline only through athletic participation is woefully misguided. One does not need to get a bloody nose to learn about perseverance. Mastering a musical instrument, for example, takes an incredible amount of perseverance, discipline, and hard work. Playing in a five-piece band requires the same teamwork skills as are necessary to participate on a basketball team. There is no difference between working together to achieve a desired sound than working together to win a ballgame. To play a song well requires the same commitment, cooperation, and discipline as executing a touchdown pass. While it takes more physical strength, conditioning, and agility to dunk a basketball, the characteristics necessary to be a successful athlete—discipline, hard work, perseverance, teamwork skills—are identical to those required to be a successful musician. In short, both music and athletics can contribute significantly to the "character" development of participants.

Music, however, offers something that highly competitive organized sports do not: a direct link between participation and intellectual development. A growing body of evidence indicates that arts instruction can significantly strengthen students' academic performance.

"Students in two Rhode Island elementary schools who were given an enriched, sequential, skill-building music program showed marked improvement in reading and math skills. Students in the enriched program who had started out behind the control group caught up to statistical equality in reading and pulled ahead in math" (Gardiner, Fox, & Knowles, 1996). A University of California (Irvine) study showed that after 8 months of keyboard lessons, preschoolers showed a 46% boost in their spatial reasoning IQ (Rauscher, Shaw, Levine, Ky, & Wright, 1994). Data from the National Education Longitudinal Study of 1988 showed that music participants received more academic honors and awards than nonmusic students, and that the percentage of music participants receiving As, As/Bs, and Bs was higher than the percentage of nonparticipants receiving those grades (National Center for Educational Statistics, 1990).

Coaches and athletic administrators, citing the large percentage of Black athletes in their programs, often argue that athletics is more effective than any other extracurricular activity in positively influencing minority students. Simply because a high percentage of athletes in high school and college athletic programs are Black does not mean that coaches and athletic administrators have cornered the market on influencing these students to achieve academically and socially. For example, a study of 811 high school students indicated that the proportion of minority students with a music teacher role model was significantly larger than for any other discipline. Thirty-six percent of these students identified music teachers as their role models, while 28% identified English teachers, 11% elementary teachers, 7% physical education/sports teachers, and 1% principals (Hamann & Walker, 1993). The athletic establishment also claims that at-risk students respond particularly well to the discipline and structure provided by athletics. Such students also respond well to music programs. A 1992 Auburn University study found significant increases in overall self-concept of at-risk children participating in an arts program that included music, movement, dramatics, and art, as measured by the Piers–Harris Children's Self-Concept Scale (Barry, 1992).

Most interesting for purposes of evaluating the type of educational investment necessary to prepare our workforce for the future, is that "the very best engineers and technical designers in the Silicon Valley industry are, nearly without exception, practicing musicians" (Venerable, 1989, p. 31).

Even the environment surrounding the conduct of a sporting event versus that of a concert suggests that investing in music would reap greater community benefits. The very nature of a sporting event tends to divide rather than bring people together, pitting opponents and spectators against each other. Sports contests invariably are trumped up to be a war for superiority between two bitter rivals. Good versus evil; right versus wrong. Music events bring people together. Everyone in a concert hall is pulling together, hoping that the musicians put on an enjoyable performance. While there is value to competition and striving to win, the current win-at-all-costs environment that permeates our competitive athletic programs is hardly healthy, serving to undermine many of the potentially positive by-products of competitive athletics.

On a somewhat less empirical level, Plato elaborated on the value of teaching music when he said, "I would teach children music, physics, and philosophy; but most importantly music, for in the patterns of music and all the arts are the keys to learning" (National Coalition for Music Education, 1997). While Plato was not opposed to athletics, he often expressed alarm at the course that athletics in ancient Greece had taken: from the purpose of developing a healthy relationship between the mind and body, to one of specialization and intense training in specific events or sports (sound familiar?). "Plato was clearly in favor of moderate physical education, but on principle he had to be critical of contemporary athletics as uneducational and impractical for the good of the individual and city" (Kyle, 1993, p. 139).

When comparing music with our current elitist, win-at-all-costs youth, interscholastic, and intercollegiate sports programs, athletics comes up short as a vehicle to prepare students to compete successfully in the workplace of the future. Yet, time and time again, when a school district or university is faced with budget cuts, it is far more likely that a program in the arts will be downsized or eliminated while the athletic program remains untouched. From an educational standpoint, such decisions are counterproductive.

REASSESSING PRIORITIES

The purpose of this chapter is not to call for the elimination of youth, high school, or college athletics. To the contrary, my belief in the educational and community value of competitive athletics is strong. Athletics can play an important role in meeting educational objectives and promoting community fitness. Competitive athletics has the potential to build character and contribute positively to the well-rounded education of our nation's youth. Sport's ability to bring a community or school together cannot be overestimated. Undoubtedly, our schools and communities would be much less vibrant without such programs.

As many of the previous authors articulated, however, sport is not educational simply because it is sport. Rather it is the environment within which sports participation occurs that influences the educational, moral, and ethical development of participants. Sport kept in the proper perspective, where the process of participation (education) is not subjugated by the game's result (winning), can be extremely positive. Sport that is overemphasized in relation to other fields of endeavor, sport that undermines educational priorities, is harmful.

The objective of this chapter is to call for an open and honest debate about the role, function, and purposes of athletics in our communities and schools. Quality education is simply too critical to continue to base policy and resource allocation decisions on emotional decrees and half-truths. As Andrew Miracle and C. Roger Rees so aptly explain in *Lessons of the Locker Room: The Myth of School Sports:*

> There is a growing movement to reassess the role of sport in American education. The movement will not be derailed by the anecdotes or personal testimony of a few true believers. It is inevitable that the search for new models will continue. It remains to be seen how most American communities will redesign the school/sport relationships. Nor is it clear what new myth about sport most Americans will come to believe. (1994, p. 226)

While some may consider the viewpoints expressed in this chapter blasphemous, they are merely a concerned warning. As much as we love sports, we must value education more. If it is determined that any element of our educational system undermines educational priorities, we must radically alter that element or eliminate it in favor of programming that promotes positive educational ideals. Make no mistake about it, our schools and colleges will survive without athletics. Most likely, sports activities would simply shift to other local sponsoring agencies, similar to the European club sports system. While our school systems would be less dynamic without athletics, the education of our populace would continue and, as some argue, might actually improve, as the focus on education would intensify.

The challenges we face in educating our children and maintaining our economic status as a world power are simply too great to invest in activities that are educationally counterproductive. The information-based, high-tech, global economy of the future requires all of us to be better educated. To effectively meet the challenges represented by these changes, we must critically assess our nation's educational priorities and outcomes. Our economic strength as a nation depends on our ability to respond to these educational challenges. No nation can become great without a well-educated populace. No nation can remain strong without an uncompromising commitment to developing its young people.

For over 100 years, we have embraced, largely without question, the notion that athletics supplements the educational missions of our schools and communities. That assumption can no longer be accepted without question. As educators, parents, and taxpayers, we must reconsider whether our tremendous investment in athletics continues to be a sound one. If, for example, we find that the intellectual and educational benefits derived from participation in a comprehensive music program outweigh the benefits of participation in athletics, perhaps we should reappropriate resources accordingly. The challenges facing our educational system and our society are too significant to continue to accept without question existing assumptions regarding athletics' educational benefits, while ignoring the benefits of other activities. To continue to blindly invest significant resources in an activity that falls far short of meeting its educational objectives is irresponsible.

A basic assumption in the athletic culture is that if an athlete is not performing up to expectations and, as a result, is not contributing in a meaningful way to the team's effort to win, the coach has a responsibility to the rest of the team to remove that player from the game or, at the very least, seriously reduce his or her playing time. Similarly, if our organized athletic programs have evolved to a point where they no longer positively contribute to our nation's educational goals, objectives, and outcomes, shouldn't the same principle apply?

REFERENCES

Barry, N. H. (1992). *Project ARISE: Meeting the needs of disadvantaged students through the arts*. Auburn University: Auburn, AL.

Flynt, W. (1990, April 25). Speech delivered at Young Men's Business Club's Man of the Year Banquet, Birmingham.

Flynt, W. (1994). *Alabama: The history of a deep south state*. Tuscaloosa: University of Alabama Press.

Gardiner, M., Fox, A., & Knowles, F. (1996, May). Learning improved by arts training. *Nature 232*, p. 284.

Hamann, D. L., & Walker, L. M. (1993). Music teachers as role models for African-American students. *Journal of Research in Music Education, 41,* 303–314.

Kyle, D. G. (1993). *Athletics in ancient Athens.* Leiden, The Netherlands: E. F. Brill.

Miracle, A. W., Jr., & Rees, C. R. (1994). *Lessons of the locker room: The myth of school sports.* Amherst, NY: Prometheus Books.

Mrozek, D. J. (1983). *Sport and American mentality 1880–1910.* Knoxville: University of Tennessee Press.

National Center for Educational Statistics. (1990). *National education longitudinal study, 1988. First follow-up.* Washington, DC: U.S. Department of Education, Office of Education Research and Improvement.

National Coalition for Music Education. (1997). *Music makes the difference* [Fact Sheet]. Reston, VA: Author.

Rauscher, F., Shaw, G., Levine, L., Ky, K., & Wright, E. (1994, August). *Music and spatial task performance: A causal relationship.* Paper presented at the American Psychological Association's 102nd annual conference, Los Angeles, CA.

Venerable, G. (1989). The paradox of the silicon savior. In E. Oddleifson (Ed.), *The case for sequential music education in the core curriculum of the public schools.* New York: The Center for the Arts in the Basic Curriculum.

12

The Rise of American Sport and the Decline of American Culture

Robert W. McCabe

It is no exaggeration to say that Americans are the leading consumers of sports in the world. In American culture, sport is an unrivaled source of entertainment and a priority for discretionary spending. For example, players and owners will receive over $17 billion over the next 8 years from Disney, CBS, and Fox for the right to bring bone-crunching NFL action to the American consumer. Those networks also plan to make some money in the process. One newspaper referred to the deal as a "jackpot." But for the consumer, and particularly the nonconsumer of professional football, the term "rip-off" might be more appropriate.

Ultimately, it would not matter if the money was an abstraction and did not have to come from somewhere. But it does matter because those enormous sums, including billions brought in by the NBA, NHL, Major League baseball, and NCAA institutions, must be paid by someone—namely, the public. Even those who do not buy tickets pay in the form of tax revenues used to fund stadium expansion or construction and team buy-out deals. And it doesn't matter that people don't buy hats or jerseys; they still pay in the form of increased product costs. Everything advertised during a game—cars, clothing, fast food, hardware, beer, household products, computers, and so on—has advertising costs built into the purchase price. The result is that everyone, not just sports fans, pays more for everything. And the cycle appears to have no end as player salaries continue to rise in step with increased television rights fees and advertising costs. Of course, many will argue that it has always been this way. After all, we live in a market economy and players, owners, manufacturers, and other parties with vested interests will charge what the market can bear.

Unfortunately, dismissing the commercial largess of today's sports marketplace overlooks a stunning and critically important fact: Modern sports are eroding American culture and undermining traditional American values essential to the well-being of our nation and its people. Sport has become the 800-pound gorilla, eating up our resources, obscuring the real problems we need to deal with, and dominating our social traditions to such an extent that our rich and diverse cultural heritage is in jeopardy. Simply consider what is on television in most homes on Thanksgiving or New Years Day, just about every Sunday, and, for that matter, many weeknight evenings.

People often find this argument to be overstated. They ask, "How can you say that sport has become a negative influence in our society?" I respond, "What does sport offer the individual that is of lasting value? What are you left with after the game is over?" While I share in people's vicarious pleasure in watching elite athletes, the merits of this activity are questionable.

As a former high school, collegiate, and professional athlete, I experienced the joys and gained the benefits of highly competitive athletics. I appreciate the positive health effects of exercise and I understand full well the entertainment value of sport. I am drawn to television sports like a moth to a flame. I am fascinated by the spectacle of big games and I know a whole lot more than I need to know about strategies, players, and coaches. I have favorite teams and athletes and I can be painfully partisan when they are doing well or failing miserably.

What worries me, however, are the things I am not doing while all of this sports excitement is going on. For example, my 5-year-old daughter is learning to read (something that many of our children do poorly) and she wants to sit with me and read "Bob Books." But Michael Jordan is putting on a show against the Knicks in Madison Square Garden. I am torn. It is difficult to turn off the television and read to my daughter without wondering what is happening in the closing minutes of the game. (He scored 42 and the Bulls won.) Admittedly, sport has a real capacity to engage people, myself included.

Unfortunately, through the combined forces of television, print media, and our appetite for leisure entertainment, sport has begun to overshadow traditional American cultural expressions and intellectual activities such as reading. Individually and collectively, we pay more than dollars for our devotion to sport. If the majority of our citizenry are rarely involved in actual physical activity, while more and more viewership creates ever more outrageous extremes at the top of the sports food chain (get ready for the two hundred million dollar athlete), then what exactly is sport doing for our culture?

An important distinction must be made at this point. My criticism of sport is not meant to discourage participation. Quite the opposite; it is the decline and corruption of broad-based local, school, and recreational athletics that alarms me (Center for Disease Control and Prevention, 1998). We watch more and more and we participate less and less, while the population, both children and adults, gets more obese with each passing year (Center for Disease Control and Prevention, 1998) as we relegate participation to a minority of elite individuals.

WHY CULTURE MATTERS

American culture is a precious achievement. Our shared identity is the result of a unique political construction emphasizing individual freedom and inclusiveness across racial, ethnic, and gender lines. Tying all of this together into a nation-state is no simple feat. Undoubtedly, sport has made notable contributions to this end. Sports icons have served as political figures and catalyzed progressive social movements. However, politically important athletes like Jackie Robinson, Muhammad Ali, or Billie Jean King are virtually nonexistent today. Presently, the major role of preeminent athletes in the national spotlight is as commercial symbols or criminal defendants.

In fact, it is hard to find solid footing for the defense of modern sport. While I endorse participation for its own sake, where does that leave the rest of the not-so-animated population? Holding the bag, but ending up with little of real value. Sport is not playing true to its original tune. The traditional virtues associated with sport included sportsmanship, education, discipline, integrity, fairness, diligence, and temperance—hardly the terms to describe the athletics we are treated to today. Instead, it is often violent, corrupt, litigious, exploitive, sexist, racially loaded, and culturally degenerative.

Try the following quiz:

1. a "facial" is?
   A. a beauty treatment
   B. a type of plastic surgery
   C. a slam dunk delivered to the head area of an opponent
2. a "crack back" block is?
   A. a chiropractic technique
   B. a sedative for childbirth
   C. a banned football maneuver

3. a "war" is?
   A. a violent political conflict
   B. a 1960's rock band
   C. a battle for position in the low post

If you answered "C" for each question, your sports viewership rating is high to dangerous. You may have been deprived of untold hours of significant development in areas such as literature, politics, the arts, and other forms of stimulation that have a lasting and cumulative value over the course of a lifetime. You may want to consider what your devotion to sport has meant to your civic, physical, and spiritual development.

My purpose is not to criticize sports viewers. I am, after all, right there with them. I wonder, however, if I had not spent so many hours playing basketball whether I might have developed a wide array of additional, and ultimately more valuable, talents. Maybe I would be able to play the piano, write software, or speak a foreign language. Maybe my relationships could be richer, my career stronger, or my grasp of politics better. While there is some satisfaction in knowing I mastered the pick and roll, I wonder what the trade-off for this skill was. Even worse, I wonder what I might have learned with the time I spent watching other people execute pick and rolls.

As we come to understand the opiate qualities of sport, we must fight back. As a start, ask the question, "What does sport do for the quality of your life?" If your first reaction is to say that playing sports adds an incredible physical and emotional element to your existence, then more power to you. There are fundamental benefits to being physical and experiencing the actual exertion of competition. People who know about the benefits of exercise have been exhorting us to simply get up and move three times a week for 30 minutes. Anything will do—walk, swim, bike, climb, dance—just do it (sound familiar?)! Unfortunately, this simple exhortation, much like "just say no," appears to be beyond the motivational capacity of the majority of Americans. Why? Maybe it is because other people do these types of athletic things so well that we are intimidated. Or, it has been so long that we don't want to look foolish or, even worse, feel foolish. Or perhaps it is just plain easier to sit there and watch while somebody else sweats it out.

Adding insult to injury, the lethargy of our physical state is dwarfed by the incapacitation sport causes in our critical thinking skills. Our spectating has promoted a high tolerance for jock babble ("I gave it 110%"), led to the deification of sports figures, fostered a multibillion dollar sports gambling enterprise (how did you do in the NCAA men's basketball pool?), and undermined the educational process from grade school to college.

SPORTS AND/OR EDUCATION

While it's a shame when Johnny can't read, it's not so bad if he can really play! In the culture we have created, children, especially boys, dream of being a sports hero rather than far more accessible alternatives such as scientist, author, educator, or entrepreneur. Further, children, particularly Black males, have fallen prey to the self-defeating belief that it is not "cool" to do well in school.

Of course, there is no equivalent negative reaction to proficiency in athletics and, over time, the two phenomena have merged so that the cultural stereotype is the "dumb jock." Excellent students are rarely considered "natural" athletes. The link, or rather the popular polarity between athleticism and intellect, is tragic. We have taken two virtues, physical and mental health, and made them culturally incompatible, making it almost unnatural for people to aspire toward both ideals. The awkwardness of this attitude is evident when we listen to television announcers rationalize Princeton's success in men's basketball.

Schools actively foster the pipedream of athletic stardom. Children are identified as "talented" in grade school, promoted on the basis of their athletic prowess, and recruited to college despite the likelihood they will never succeed academically. Nearly half (47%) of all male athletes who participated in NCAA Division I athletics between 1984 and 1991 never graduated from college (National Collegiate Athletic Association, 1997). This, despite financial scholarships and specialized academic support.

Major colleges and universities compromise their academic values by enrolling students they would never dream of admitting except for their athletic skills (Knight Foundation Commission on Intercollegiate Athletics, 1991). Saddled with adults who read like children, many institutions devote substantial resources to academic support programs and develop courses of study that are less strenuous and thus less valuable. The result is that the regular student body, their families, and taxpayers supporting public institutions are squeezed for fees to help pay for facilities and academic scholarships that have little to do with academics. In the end, athletes do not graduate and school administrators find themselves wrestling with an athletic department that undermines core academic principles.

More than one college president has found himself out of a job after a tangle with a high-profile coach. And what does it say about institutional priorities when the football or basketball coach makes four or five times more money than the president? Faculty think the whole arrangement stinks, as do coaches of the so-called "minor" sports. There is, however, little they can do about it. A crush of support in the community, a commitment to competitive traditions, conference and divisional affiliations, and the pursuit of big paydays in football bowl games or the NCAA basketball tournament provide incentives that fuel an athletics arms race that pits one institution against the other.

In the end, we have made a very clear and culturally significant choice. Academics can and will be sacrificed for athletics. This is a serious indictment of higher education's integrity, a remarkable compromise of values by many of the leading educational institutions in the world, and a significant blow to our future educational and economic prosperity.

Higher education is the intellectual engine of the country. It is the crucial link between the development of skilled workers and the nation's private sector. Higher education is also the driving force behind the development of curriculum and educational standards for elementary, middle, and high schools. The educational reforms made in many primary and secondary school systems are dictated by the nation's colleges and universities. If technical skills or a grasp of basic elements of writing or literature is essential to success in college, then feeder schools emphasize these subjects.

Unfortunately, while higher education spurs the intellectual innovation of primary and secondary schools, it also sets an appalling example for the practice of school sports. When it comes to athletics, many schools discard their ethical norms for the sake of competitive success and athletic revenues. Academic benchmarks such as validity, integrity, and progressive innovation, essential to the practice of physics, biology, or any other academic discipline, simply are ignored in the case of athletics. Instead, higher education models a bottom-line mentality in athletics and primary and secondary schools follow suit.

The result is a growing trend in school sports toward greater sports specialization at younger ages, the "passing through" from grade to grade of academically unqualified athletes, and a general buy-in with the darker side of higher education's sports system. School programs that foster broad-based participation and emphasize sports as a component of the educational process are being undermined. Many public schools have dropped recreational programs, physical education classes, and junior varsity teams. Instead, their focus is on the development of a competitively successful elite group of athletes at the expense of the larger student body.

If school-based programs are not being used for the physical and emotional development of a majority of students, what then are they for? I doubt anyone is comfortable with school sports becoming a feeder system for major college athletic programs. Further, since sports in public schools are funded by the families of all students, shouldn't high participation levels be the ultimate goal? Unfortunately, a competitive ethic, borrowed from collegiate and professional sports, has convinced people that playing something is worthwhile only if done at an elite level. Playing for fun, good health, camaraderie, and the development of lifelong habits of physical activity is not highly valued. Many children stop playing because they know they cannot be the best and opportunity is exclusive (Tye, 1997). In sum, sport in our culture has evolved to the point where there is little support for participation simply for the joy of playing and the subtler benefits that accrue to the participant over time.

SPORTS, VIOLENCE, GENDER, AND RACE

While the stupefying costs for sports entertainment, sloth in the majority of the nation's spectators, and a compromise of our intellect and academic institutions are reasons enough to be concerned about sports' influence in our society, there are more insidious issues that must be addressed—specifically, the links between sports, violence, racism, and sexism.

Professor John Hoberman of the University of Texas, in his book, *Darwin's Athletes* (1997), maintains that America's fixation with Black athletes promulgates a prejudiced view of biological difference. In addition to arguing that sport stereotypes Blacks and has merged Black athletes into a gross caricature by portraying them as "athlete-gangster-rappers," he contends that sport has contributed to a peer-group culture of anti-intellectualism among Black adolescents (Hoberman, 1997, p. xviii).

What is the social dynamic when televised sports such as basketball and football feature a dominant Black presence while the viewing public is largely White? Are Black and White Americans making assumptions of physical difference based on race? Perhaps even more disturbing, are Black and White Americans making assumptions about the intellectual capacity of Blacks based on their perceptions of Black athletes? Given the racial legacy of Black and White relations in this country, there can be little doubt that sport provides some people with a validation of racist views.

In my own work with athletic staff and student-athletes at Division I colleges and universities, I have found that sports participation can promulgate negative stereotypes and lead to prejudice and discrimination. For example, if you ask Black male student-athletes at Division I schools to describe how they are perceived by the student body, a disturbing pattern emerges. They believe White students see them as dangerous, aggressive, dishonest, and less intelligent. Further, Black student-athletes believe that White students think they are on campus only to play sports, and receive preferential academic treatment and other benefits not available to the general student body.

However, if you ask Black student-athletes about their actual experience, you get an entirely different picture. For example, Black student-athletes are usually highly motivated students, are very wary of conflicts and the danger they associate with any sort of interaction with police, and often describe their undergraduate experience as isolated and alienating (American Institutes for Research, 1989). If the general student body thinks Black student-athletes have it so good, why then are Black student-athletes finding campus life so hostile?

It is a case of perception becoming reality. Stereotypical racial roles in athletics lead to prejudicial attitudes that in turn manifest themselves in racist and discriminatory behaviors. In the minds of Whites, the Black athlete's success in sport comes at a price, and the historical trade-off has been intelligence.

In fact, it is the pursuit of commercial success in athletics that has led to some of the most harmful stereotyping of Black athletes. Consider the advertisements featuring prominent Black athletes such as Shaquille O'Neal, Charles Barkley, Bruce Smith, Shawn Kemp, Hakeem Olajuwan, Nate Newton, or David Robinson. Several themes emerge. First, many of these athletes have no dialogue in their own commercials; they don't speak. Second, the visuals often portray their athletic capabilities in violent tones. And third, through the use of sound effects, lighting, wardrobe, and popular pseudonyms, the athlete is often transformed into a form of snarling, predatory animal. The net effect is a bestial portrayal that mirrors the historical racist presentation of the Black male as a brute.

Michael Jordan, by far the most successful commercial spokesman among today's superstars, stands as a notable exception to the general method of marketing Black male athletes. In his ads he is almost always speaking, his athletic image is one of grace over force, he has remained utterly human, and he appears as a promoter for an extremely wide range of products. In fact, Jordan's image transcends race and he operates in a commercial medium quite different than his peers. He is articulate, nonthreatening, and sensitive. In short, he is humanized while many of his contemporaries must conform to coarser, less flattering roles to capitalize on their visibility.

Like Jordan, the popular White superstar has a positive, friendly marketing persona. White athletes like Joe Montana, Steve Young, Brett

Favre, Larry Bird, Cal Ripkin, John Elway, and Wayne Gretzky are featured in commercials that portray them as articulate, thoughtful, honest, and nonthreatening. In fact, for some of these athletes (particularly quarterbacks), the physical danger they face in their sport is represented in their commercials by aggressive Black athletes.

In addition to being an expression of racial attitudes, sport is significant in the formation of our public conception of gender. To a significant extent, the surge in women's athletic opportunities and popularity is positive. In the almost 30 years since the passage of Title IX brought legal impetus to providing sports opportunities for females, participation opportunities have flourished. During the late 1990s, the popularity of women's sports were boosted by the highly visible success of the U.S. women's Olympic basketball, soccer, and hockey teams. The formation of two professional basketball leagues for women, as well as the planned development of professional leagues for women in softball, soccer, and hockey, all indicate that women's sports will become a fixture of the sports marketplace.

Such growth, however, overshadows aspects of women's sports that raise serious questions. For example, if the development of women's sports parallels that of men's, will we see a replication of a money-centered, market-oriented sports culture? Will Black female athletes receive the same stereotypical, culturally biased marketing opportunities currently offered to their male counterparts? Will women's athletics, like virtually all entertainment activities featuring women, use sexual attractiveness as a marketing tool? This last concern has already been raised with respect to the marketing of professional women's beach volleyball.

There is little question regarding the marketing direction men's athletics has taken. Men's sports have become increasingly violent (a trend women can emulate at their own peril). Worse, sports promotions use that violence to establish credibility and draw fans. In the NFL, it's "smashmouth" football and promotional videos of brutal hits. In the NBA, it is the hyper-aggressive defense, fouls that border on assault, and the marketing of huge men with even bigger attitudes. In hockey, it is the traditional fare of jarring checks and sanctioned fights with a sprinkling of high sticks and team brawls. Not to be outdone, Major League baseball has batters charging the mound and fracases with all players joining in.

While violence in a broad context is great marketing, ugly incidents have become more common and harder to explain away as the irrational act of the individual player. It is a delicate job trying to balance nearly hysterical intensity with self-restraint. For many athletes, the lines have blurred and they find themselves in the center of whirling controversies, at once admonished for their actions but popular and wildly compensated nonetheless. More than a few athletes have built their professional reputations on being a bit hair-trigger and dangerous.

This rise in aggression and violence within traditional sports is troublesome. However, the growth of fringe sports whose appeal seems entirely predicated on testing the boundaries of athletic behavior is downright alarming, for example, the modern incarnation of professional wrestling and the savage ultimate fighting contests. It is also interesting to note that in addition to the ultra-violent qualities of these sports, they feature degrading roles for women. At these events, women play terrified sex objects, scandalous vixens, and other inferior characters in submission to aggressive, dangerous men. One can not help but wonder if there is some connection between these extremes and the epidemic of violence currently endured by American women.

SEARCHING FOR COMMON SENSE

In the end, it is very difficult to prove any causal link between sports and negative or deviant social behavior. The role of sports, if indeed it plays one, in exacerbating our problems with violence and crime, education, race, and gender, or any other national concern, is difficult to ascertain. Perhaps it would be more constructive to step back and pose a series of questions and let common sense sort things out. Is sport playing a positive role in the fair distribution of resources within our society? Is sport supporting the educational process? Are more people actively engaging in athletics for their health? Is sport promoting racial or gender equity?

On a more personal level, ask yourself, Is sport making a long-term contribution to the quality of your life? If so, you should have some tangible benefits you can point to. Are you healthier? Is sport bringing your family together? Is sport helping you contribute to your community? Is sport broadening your conception of racial and gender equality? Finally, what other forms of entertainment and activities do you engage in besides viewing sports? Do interests like literature, museums, film, travel, politics, crafts, or the sciences constitute the bulk of your leisure activities?

Sorting all of this out can be difficult. To begin, use the following quiz to test yourself:

1. Name three members of the 1997–98 Chicago Bulls.
2. Name three members of the United States Supreme Court.

3. Name the winning team in the 1997 World Series.
4. Name your two current representatives in the U.S. Senate.
5. In football, when a team is awarded a safety, how many points do they get?
6. Who won Pulitzer Prizes for fiction in 1982 and 1991 for his portrayals of an ex-high school star athlete?
7. In hockey, what is the violation for passing the puck across two lines on the ice called?
8. In Congress, the tactic for stalling a bill to prevent a vote is called?
9. Name the annual award given to college football's premier player.
10. Name the international award distributed yearly to individuals who have most benefited humankind in physics, chemistry, medicine-physiology, literature, and promotion of peace.

If you had an easy time answering the odd numbered questions, you demonstrated a good grasp of sports trivia. (Odd answers: 1. See Bulls roster/box score, 3. Florida Marlins, 5. Two, 7. Icing, 9. The Heisman.) If you struggled with the even numbered questions, you have a questionable grasp of simple civics and other socially relevant information. (Even answers: 2. See Supreme Court members list, 4. See your state's elected senators, 6. John Updike, 8. A filibuster, 10. The Nobel awards.) Even a simple test like this can give you insight into your values as evidenced by what you embrace as common knowledge. Unfortunately, I am convinced that most Americans, particularly males, would perform at a much higher level on the sports portion than the civic or cultural items. This is disturbing because civic and cultural phenomena ultimately determine the quality of our lives.

CONCLUSION

I have focused on the juxtaposition of sports and civic issues because I believe our obsession with sports is detrimental to our cultural evolution. Modern sports need to be depopularized on the national level and prioritized on the local level, with participation as the key indicator of success. I do not advocate any direct measures such as legislation or other governmental or institutional means. Rather, balancing sports participation and viewing with other activities is a personal choice, an extension of one's own character and goals. In most cases, I believe people simply have not evaluated their own sports behaviors critically. A reappraisal of the relevance of sport would solve a lot of the problems I have identified so far.

For example, reduced interest in professional sports would result in a shrinking sports market, smaller contracts for athletes, and less revenue for owners. Fewer dollars and fans would lower the profile of professional sport as a cultural force. This would mitigate the impact of some of the social influences of sport that are problematic. People would make entertainment choices that could benefit more educational institutions such as museums, theaters, and national parks. People could elect to participate more and enjoy direct benefits to their health. It is a simple scenario wherein people make sports more personal, local, and balanced in the context of a more diverse and stimulating life. Of course, if it is so simple, why don't more people do it?

People are highly susceptible to the hyper-commercial spectacle of big-time sporting events. Sports marketing is pervasive and extremely effective. In effect, sport presents an illusion of importance. Players and owners contrive to perpetuate sport as an important activity. Newspapers, news broadcasts, and television shows present contract battles between players and owners as real news. It is good conflict theater (very appealing to males), but in fact players and owners are in collusion, and the public's gullibility is reflected in today's sports salaries and the cost of a ticket to any professional event.

The noted historian, Doris Kearns-Goodwin (1998), believes our current civic condition is characterized by low political involvement, low attentiveness to political issues, and a failure to care about each other. This is a threat to our national well-being, and I'm afraid that sport has offered itself as an illusory alternative to involvement in substantive activities that make life meaningful. Any real change in this state of affairs will be the result of millions of individual choices, the foremost of which will be your own.

REFERENCES

American Institutes for Research. (1989, March). *Studies of intercollegiate athletes: Report No. 3. The experiences of black intercollegiate athletes at NCAA Division I institutions*. Palo Alto, CA: National Collegiate Athletic Association.

Maslen, B. L., & Maslen, J. Bob books. New York: Scholastic.

Center for Disease Control and Prevention. (1998). *Morbidity and mortality weekly report*. Atlanta.

Hoberman, J. (1997). *Darwin's athletes: How sport has damaged black america and preserved the myth of race*. New York: Houghton Mifflin.

Kearns-Goodwin, D. (1998, January, 2). *The news hour with Jim Lehrer* [WGBH TV]. Boston.

Knight Foundation Commission on Intercollegiate Athletics. (1991). *Keeping faith with the student-athlete: A new model for inter-collegiate athletics.* Charlotte, NC: Knight Foundation.

National Collegiate Athletic Association. (1997). *1997 NCAA Division I graduation rates report.* Overland Park, KS: Author.

Tye, L. (1997, September 28). Playing under pressure. *The Boston Globe,* p. F-1.

13

The Pedestals Are Vacant

Bill Curry

Ozymandias

I met a traveler from an antique land
Who said: Two vast and trunckless legs of stone
Stand in the desert. Near them, on the sand,
Half sunk, a shattered visage lies, whose frown,
And wrinkled lip, and sneer of cold command,
Tell that its sculptor well those passions read
Which yet survive, stamped on these lifeless things,
The hand that mocked them, and the heart that fed;
And on the pedestal these words appear:
"My name is Ozymandias, king of kings;
Look on my works, ye Mighty, and despair!"
Nothing beside remains. Round the decay
Of that colossal wreck, boundless and bare,
The lone and level sands stretch far away.

Percy Bysshe Shelley

The vision came with a clarity so pronounced that it felt like a bolt of lightning, full of electricity and ozone. It was 1993, and I stood at Olympia, Greece, site of the original Olympic Games. We were on a tour of the area and I felt like George Patton when he surveyed ancient battlefields. "I have been here before," reverberated through my mind. I have spent all of my life on the fields of competition.

There was a primeval depth about my response, a sense that some basic part of me was anchored by, linked with, the ancient gods and participants in this most serious of competitions. When I repressed or dismissed it with ideas and ideals of more and better substance, I found it creeping back again and again, reminding me, "We belong here—we are part of you." I wondered, "Did I fall in the dust of Olympia long ago? Why am I so compelled, even driven, to come back to this violent world as if I would die without it?" I don't know, and it is probably best to leave the subject with another quote attributed to Patton: "I love it—God help me, I do love it so."

"These empty pedestals were reserved for statues of the Olympic champions," our guide emphatically stated. "The Olympics were intended to instruct the participants in the virtue and joy of competition. If any dishonor were discovered, the guilty was humiliated by having his statue replaced with that of Zeus, so all would know that he was not a champion, but an imposter." There was the clear indication that Zeus was not happy, and that the big fellow would be looking up the cheater for some serious retribution.

It was easy for me, in fact quite comfortable, to imagine the erstwhile Greek Olympic Committee addressing the athletes, while thousands of spectators mixed and mingled to see and be seen. "Young men, you are the flower of the Greek civilization, the best of the best. You represent every corner of the Greek world. You come from as far away as Egypt, Marseilles, and Africa. You are all free men—there are no slaves or women among you. If you are well trained, and prepared to compete honorably, you are in the right place. If not, leave now."

As I absorbed all of this, standing where the runners took their odd-looking stances to begin the games' first event, I was suddenly smitten with the sense that these great, naked paragons of virtue had been betrayed. Their innocence and discipline had been replaced by my generation's greed and self-promotion. I wondered and wandered around the hallowed ground. How had we let nobility slip away? How could we, the descendants of this pure amateur breed, have become so tarnished?

The guide continued, informing us that the original Olympics, circa 776 B.C., had deep religious meaning, featuring a logical, beautiful progression, beginning with sacrificial expenditure of energy to honor Zeus. The contestants were honest, diligent, probably even loyal, trustworthy, and brave. They did not cheat, think evil thoughts, or even wear jocks. They were tough and didn't care who won or what the rewards for victory were. They simply loved their religion, loved to train, and loved to compete for the sheer joy of competition.

That is the tale the guide told. And that is what I unquestioningly accepted.

OLYMPIC REALITY

We are all capable of occasionally falling prey to laminated thinking, best characterized by the bumper sticker, "Don't confuse me with the facts— my mind is made up." But in this case, the truth is too compelling, well documented, and obvious to dodge. As I began to poke around for further proof of the image the guide had encouraged and I so willingly had embraced, what I discovered was that the pedestals were vacant. Like Ozymandias, the "immortals" of the ancient Olympics learned how fleeting and illusory fame is, even the stone variety.

Yes, these guys were naked; yes, they were well-conditioned; and yes, they competed like hell. Beyond that however, the whole system was all too familiar.

While the placing of an olive wreath upon the victor's head fits comfortably into our preconceived, self-serving notions of what "pure sport should be about," the facts tell us that there was nothing pure or amateur about ancient Olympic athletes. Much like athletes today, a god-like status was conferred upon the victors, complete with huge cash bonuses, prizes, and inducements. And since the prevailing religious thought of the day did not provide for an afterlife, the notion of immortality took on a meaning we cannot fathom. "Nobility and valor, greed and avarice, glory and glorification, unions and contract negotiations, heroics and heroization, corruption and vilification. . . . In short, nearly every aspect of athletics we know today existed already in that distant [Greek] but kindred world" (Miller, 1991, p. 201). "There has never been any evidence for amateurism in ancient Greece. . . . All Greek athletes from the start collected as much prize money as they could win" (Young, 1988, p. 62).

Sons of Athens who won Olympic events were provided free meals for life. It was not unusual for athletes to fight to the death, for to lose was simply too devastating. "They went back to their mothers without delight, creeping through narrow alleys." This, according to Pindar, poet of the ancient games (The First Olympics, 1997). I know that feeling well, as do all driven competitors. Thus, that Greek Olympic Committee member may very well also have said, "Most importantly, hear this: Winning is everything. You must win. There are no awards for second or third place."

With my heroes off their pedestals, perhaps now I can get on with reality.

Reality is that our tawdry preoccupation with children's games, our misplaced value systems, and our gross rewards for athletes are neither new nor a recurring progression of historical cycles. Reality is rather that this is a constant, a fact of the human condition. Only the expressions differ.

Bob McCabe suggests in Chapter 12 that sports may have no real value in our culture and that our energy would be better spent in contemplation and pursuit of loftier forms of art. John Gerdy goes one step further with a recommendation: Let's change direction completely and establish more and better music programs in lieu of athletics. Reality seems to remind us that people do not care if sports are generally destructive, and that endowments for public education would face stern challenges if the big contributors were invited to a concert rather than a luxury box on the 50-yard line.

LEGENDS IN OUR OWN MINDS

In 1971, I was the center on the world champion Baltimore Colts. It was heady stuff; you could say our "statues were on pedestals." The Super Bowl, after its fifth edition, was beginning to resemble today's bacchanal, and some of us were beginning to see ourselves as remnants of Olympia, legends in our own minds. In training camp the following July, I dressed next to a promising rookie from a prominent football power. This youngster was a good player but he was obviously nervous, visibly shaken about his first practice with John Mackey, Johnny Unitas, Mike Curtis, and others. As the old veteran, I thought I should welcome him and perhaps comfort him.

As we dressed, I asked, "What was your major in school?"

He responded, "Football."

I chuckled at his wit, then pressed him, "Seriously, what did you study?"

He replied, "I'm not kidding—football was my major."

"What does that mean?" Now I was really curious.

"Well, I only took electives. The coaches changed my major every year so I didn't have to take tough courses—I just took electives like philosophy of basketball, physical education, and.... I think maybe I took an English course one time; I'm not sure."

"How long would it take to get a degree if you returned to school?" I asked.

"Three and one-half years, I guess. Maybe more."

I wondered aloud whether they would return him to scholarship.

"Of course not. My eligibility expired," he said.

"Let me get this straight. You helped them fill the stadium, win championships, and made the coach rich and famous. What did you get in return?" I asked.

"I get the chance to play on the team with you guys," he responded.

I mumbled something like, "I hope so," and went to practice.

He did not make our team, and I have been haunted by that conversation. At Georgia Tech, under Bobby Dodd, we were forced to attend every class, expected to graduate, and required to take chemistry, physics, calculus, and many other demanding subjects. Over 90% of our players earned their degrees. I had been foolish enough to think our program was the norm.

LIVING ON THE EDGE

During the same training camp, one of life's serendipities occurred, a once-in-a-career moment. George Plimpton showed up. What a man! Plimpton was not so much a sportswriter as he was a writer about people in sports. A scholarly sort, he was taken by the feelings engendered in competition, so much so that he invented "participatory journalism." He reasoned that if one wished to write about how it feels to box, what better research than to box a champ like Archie Moore? This he did, along with numerous other forays into our bizarre athletic world. On this occasion, he was to "participate" as a quarterback on our team in an exhibition game. The opponent was to be the Detroit Lions, with whom he had spent a training camp, and about whom he wrote a hilarious best seller, *Paper Lion.*

We quickly became fast friends. I greatly admired his unique form of courage. Here he was, 44 years of age, an angular 6'4", a bit awkward, joining every drill. The players progressed from curiosity to amusement, and then to respect. He was there to shoot a one-hour television special to be aired nationally, "Plimpton, The Great Quarterback Sneak." He wanted to experience all of the agony, dehydration, fatigue, and loneliness of training camp.

He became attached to me by necessity. I was the only veteran center, and the rookie usually jammed George's fingers with his snaps. So when George was called in to scrimmages with the second unit, he usually came up with a tremulous, "Where is that Curry fellow? You remember, number 50 I think it is." We worked and talked, worked and talked, until our dialogue became an analysis of the violent world of football. His mind was so keen, his insights so profound, that for the first time I found myself in the role of apologist for my profession.

When his big day arrived, we performed at the half of an exhibition game with the Lions. It was held at the "Big House" in Ann Arbor, Michigan, home of the University of Michigan Wolverines. The largest crowd in NFL history, 104,000 people, gathered to witness the spectacle. Could a "normal" person make his way in the football arena? George's appeal in all of his ventures stemmed from this sort of speculation.

George did fine. We had a first down (they hit him late), he almost completed a slant pass, and he handled the ball well. He also deflected what we call "trash talk" in today's parlance. The Lions were the masters of trash talk circa 1971. And, to add to the party atmosphere, they had held George up for more money just before kickoff.

When we filed in afterward, George sat dejectedly in the back of the locker room, his chin in his hands. When he saw me approaching, his eyes flashed. "That was the most disgusting experience of my entire life! You guys are sick! I have never experienced such hatred!"

A neat wrap on his four down experience, I thought. I grinned and said, "That's not hatred, George, that is intensity; we are competitors." He was inconsolable and remained unmoved when we next spoke. I offered the regular bromides about catharsis, teamwork, and diligence, then listened to him until he said that we ought to write it all down, do a book, make something of our discussions. *One More July* was our collaborative effort, published in 1977.

The gist of our book was captured in the title. Those of us drawn to combative competition are born to this kind of life. It seems as if we do not so much choose to compete, as that we are chosen. If sport is indeed "on the edge" in the educational process, perhaps the reason is that its basic components, the participants themselves, crave the precipice, live on various edges, because they must. *One More July* refers to my predisposition to regulate every aspect of my life by the landmark reporting date for football training camps.

By the time George and I were contemplating a title, I was looking beyond football, and a business friend hit me between the eyes with my history. "Bill, if you really want to sell insurance, you will do well. But if you think you can dabble in it while you prepare for one more July, you will be very disappointed. What you must do is find your next July and go for that."

FINDING "BLISS," DISCARDING ILLUSIONS

The great philosopher Joseph Campbell (1989) writes compellingly of "Bliss." When one finds, or is found by, one's bliss, then there is no choice but to pursue it. Campbell postulates that anyone can find his bliss by simply identifying the activity in which he loses track of time. Tales of prodigious accomplishments abound in which the accomplishers had no sense of time or space and could not rest until the deed was done. Bliss in sport has been called many things—we seek the "zone," swing for the "sweet spot," or drive ourselves for "peak performance."

The kid from the football powerhouse did not care, could not have cared, about his diploma because he was utterly focused on the source of his kind of bliss. Moral or immoral, the system accommodated him, probably used him. But who is to say he did not seek and use such a system because it was his destiny? Scholarly George Plimpton placed himself in our world, earned our respect, then was horrified by the sheer obsession he sensed. Perhaps we should not be surprised by either response, but rather see the whole mess for what it is, realizing that these are two archetypes of response systems.

For my part, losing track of time has meant a series of Julys from 1955 through 1996. Yes, July 1997 was the first time in 42 years that I did not report for training camp. There are no words to describe my feelings. Suffice it to say that 42 years is a long time to remain immersed in any brand of bliss. The statement "football demands every gut in a man's body," is not a coaching platitude if one is in for the long haul. It is rather a statement of fact. I suppose the obvious question here would involve the search for that delicate line between bliss and obsessive-compulsive pathology. I cannot answer that one, but I can offer a unique perspective.

If we accept the premise that a certain obsession with athletics is inevitable, and that there are young people who are essentially destined to compete on our fields and courts, if we recognize that the burning desire to win is potentially destructive but, nonetheless, a force of nature, if we bring more of the hypocrisy into the light of day, then we can at least be honest about what we are doing. At best, we can combine those realities to forge a new and better model, discarding illusions about the good old days or any days, for that matter.

FOOTBALL IS LIFE

Sport was the main occupation for all of us, and continued to be mine
for a long time. That is where I had my only lesson in ethics.
                              Albert Camus (Plimpton, 1992, p. 466)

Football is just life marked off in one hundred yards.
                                                        Bill Badgett

Albert Camus, the French existentialist author, and Bill Badgett, my high school football coach, did not know each other. I doubt seriously that they would have communicated well. But on one point they were both public and adamant. One learns how to behave—how to live—from athletic experience. Coach Badgett was constantly ridiculed (behind his back) for his relentless preaching of the one-hundred-yard life experience. But on reflection, I still feel the powerful lessons he hammered into us. They *were* ethical, they *were* true-to-life, and they *do* abide.

Consider the lot of short, chubby, 13-year-old Bill Curry. It was spring practice and I hated football. It was cold and rainy, and everything hurt. To make matters worse, I was lined up as linebacker against the first string. When our 200-pound fullback, Roy Betsill, crashed through the line, my 130-pound body shuttered, ducked, and waved him on to his customary touchdown. Not unusual, and not nearly as painful as the alternative—tackling Roy. The whistle blew, I returned to the huddle, and only then did I notice the ominous silence—everyone was looking at me. Now *that* was unusual. Coach Badgett stared with that riveting presence only he could generate, and said quietly, "Run the same play again. Don't block Curry. Bill, tackle Roy Betsill. Do you hear me?" Terror . . . everyone watching . . . more than a few smirks . . . little sympathy . . . a whole lot of "better you than me." Roy came, I ducked, he ran over me, up one side and down the other. I got up, checked for broken bones, and was relieved to find none, only to hear, "Run it again. Bill, I said to tackle Roy." No yelling, no threats, just the power of the moment. He might as well have told me to tackle the Nancy Hanks diesel train that roared through our little town. I just couldn't do it. That was my thought. But it was not Bill Badgett's. "Again," he said, "and again, and again." Now my nose bled and I wept, big hot tears of humiliation, fear, and . . . anger? Somewhere from my essence a more powerful voice spoke, perhaps for the first time. "He is going to keep you here forever. You have a choice in this matter." It was me; I bent my knees, squared my shoulders, and drilled Roy Betsill in the middle of his washboard abdomen with all my might. I drove him over onto his back. He smiled, and my teammates cheered, ran, and hugged me. Badgett almost smiled. I was hooked. Was that child abuse? I think not.

Ten years later, I sat in the Green Bay Packers locker room with a splitting headache. It was a Monday morning following a Saturday night exhibition game, and I had received a concussion against the Pittsburgh Steelers. We players thought it was funny, although we know better now. Our coach, Vince Lombardi, entered and called Ray Nitchske and me. Ray was our All-Pro middle linebacker, and well known as one of the toughest men in the league. "I want you two to dress in pads and go to the field with Coach Wietecha," he said. That's all. No instructions.

When we reached the field, we were told to stretch, which we did. Then, for the only time in all my years of football, we engaged in a full-speed, one-on-one drill with no other players present. After several smashes, the results of which I do not recall, we were stopped and returned to the locker room. The next day, the final cut was made, meaning the roster for the season had been selected. Only then did it dawn on me—the final phase of my "physical" was to see if I would smash my head into a powerful linebacker! No doctor, no lights in the eyes, no EEGs—just a linebacker. Was that good? Was that courageous? Who should receive blame? The answer is clear. I was a grown man and understood the system. I crossed that fine line of my own volition. Reflecting on the moment, it seems now that I was drawn, as the moth to the flame; I could not do otherwise. Most professional athletes make a similar decision at some moment. We praise them, reward them, even worship them if their timing is right.

So there exists this alchemy of horror and beauty, elusive in its nature, luring and repelling in turn, but always *affecting*, touching deeply those who linger in its field of potential. There are no simple answers for this one. I have alternately been rewarded and burned so may times as to defy description. If football condones violence, it also rewards compassion and empathy. If it creates superstars, it also promotes unselfishness and teamwork. If it is given to unholy fanaticism, it also is enjoyed by the thoughtful and reserved. If it produces chaos, it also demands remarkable order and planning. If it has been abused by the plantation mentality, it also has forced cultural diversity and the embracing of all types of people. If it has an obvious sexist bent, it also has funded much of the good work in women's athletics. If it undermines the educational process, it also has caused thousands to pursue education when they might not have done so otherwise. If it has retarded maturity, it also has made men of boys in the arena, yea the crucible of stamina, perseverance, pure physical and mental toughness. If it has fostered dishonesty off the field, it has forced pure honesty within the white lines, where total commitment is a requisite for survival. If it has shattered bones and snapped ligaments, it also has strengthened muscles and shaped young bodies to be lean and fit for life. If it occasionally has paid homage to the flash-in-the-pan talent of the individual, it also has consistently included the unsung, untalented grunt who knows diligence and persistence. If it has a corrosive effect on civility and other important values, it also has provided powerful examples of the greatest virtues, pure love and sacrificial giving. If it has promoted unhealthy violence, it also has been the only place many aggressive youngsters could find expression and catharsis. It is magnificent, terrible, beautiful, hideous, pristine, and corrupt. It is . . . well, football. It is life.

Bill Badgett was on the mark.

REFERENCES

Campbell, J. (1989). *The power of myth: Dialogue with Bill Moyers.* Montauk, NY: Mystic Fire Video.

The First Olympics. (1997). [Documentary shown on The History Channel. Sources interviewed were John Mikalson, University of Virginia, and Thomas Scanlon, University of California, Riverside].

Miller, S. G. (1991). *Arete: Greek sports from ancient sources.* Berkeley: University of California Press.

Plimpton, G. (1977). *One more July: A football dialogue with Bill Curry.* New York: Harper & Row.

Plimpton, G. (ed.). (1992). *The Norton book of sports.* New York: Norton.

Shelley, P. B. (1959). Ozymandias. In G. B. Harrison (Ed.), *Major British writers* (Vol. 2, p. 254). New York: Harcourt, Brace & World.

Young, D.C. (1988). How the amateurs won the Olympics. In W. J. Rashke (Ed.), *Archaeology of the Olympics* (pp. 55–75). Madison: University of Wisconsin Press.

Concluding Remarks

The purpose of this collection of chapters is not to "tear down" athletics, but to strengthen it. Each of the authors believes very strongly in athletics' potential to contribute to educational processes in vital ways. All are "products" of the system, having been shaped by the lessons learned on the fields and courts of play. It is because of their genuine belief in the value of athletic participation that they voice their concerns. Having been so intimately involved in athletics, they all know that there is nothing intrinsically educational about hitting a ball or tackling an opponent. These are merely physical acts. They know that it is the environment within which these acts occur that influences the educational and personal development of the participants. They also know that the relationship between athletics and education has become badly skewed.

Youth, high school, and college sports programs today are radically different from those of 20 or even 10 years ago—more money at stake, widespread television exposure, and more pressure on youth to perform and on coaches to win. These changes have made the increasingly critical questions regarding sport as a vehicle to promote positive educational outcomes much more difficult to answer.

The fact that there are no simple answers should not stop us from asking the questions. The challenges facing our nation are too daunting to trivialize them. Education's role in addressing those problems is too critical to dismiss them. And the influence of sport within our educational system is too strong to ignore these questions by blindly accepting the status quo. In other words, sport is not simply fun and games. Its cultural impact is pervasive, touching each and every one of us. The way in which sports programs are conducted, the values they promote, and the messages they send, have a critical influence on the educational welfare of our country.

The fact that sport's influence is so extensive must not discourage efforts to hold athletic programs accountable for the outcomes they produce. To unquestioningly accept whatever consequences our sports programs produce simply because sport is "too big" and the win-at-all-costs mentality that drives it so ingrained in the fabric of our nation's psyche that "it will never change," is educationally irresponsible. People, organizations, and yes, even an institution as "sacred" as sport, can change. After all, there was a time when the thought of putting a man on the moon, or tearing down the Berlin Wall, was inconceivable. And there was a moment when a young, skinny, Bill Curry believed it was impossible to tackle big Roy Betsill.

If we are going to continue to invest heavily in an activity that is justified, in large part, upon its ability to produce positive educational outcomes, then, as in any educational community, the search for truth must guide our evaluation of the effectiveness with which it meets its objectives. As concerned educators, parents, and citizens, we must continually evaluate whether athletics does what it claims to do.

If athletics does in fact contribute positively to meeting our nation's educational objectives, perhaps we should invest more heavily in it. If not, we must not only rethink how it can, but we must have the courage to follow through with policies and actions that support the sanctity of the educational process rather than behavior that affects only the final score. If we lack such coverage, it is only a matter of time before athletics "loses its edge" as a vital educational resource. And if it does; if the relationship between sport and education becomes so weak; if athletics evolves to a point where its influence on education becomes more negative than positive, we will have no choice but to take action accordingly.

There are many elements of our nation's athletic "system" that must be reconsidered and changed, particulary sport that is conducted within our educational system or sport that is justified primarily upon educational grounds. As a coach, educator, athletic administrator, parent, or member of the media, it is easy to simply resign oneself to the fact that the system is too big and ingrained and thus will never change. It is easy to simply accept the "realities" of the system and make no effort to change them.

As a result, it is easy to think that no one is terribly interested in changing the way sport is conducted in America. I do not believe that to be the case. Most people not only know what is the right thing to do, but want to do it. An increasing number of Americans believe that the importance placed upon sports at the youth, high school, and college levels is wildly out of proportion and, as a result, is having a negative effect on our educational system.

What, then, can an individual do to make a difference? Can an individual change the system? While it may be rare that an individual single-handedly "changes the world," individuals can have a positive impact, can contribute in meaningful ways to a collective effort to influence change. Whether a parent, coach, educator, or athletic administrator, you can make a difference. You can change those whom you touch, the programs you or your children are involved in, or the organization for which you work. Like the "sixth man" who comes off the bench and ignites a team with his or her hustle or by scoring a few quick baskets, you can lift and inspire those around you. As Bob McCabe points out in Chapter 12, the choice to do so is a personal one. You must decide to take a stand. You must decide to do the educationally responsible thing. As a parent, you must decide to challenge your local youth sports leagues to, as Bob Bigelow suggested in Chapter 1, "give sports back to the children." As a youth sports coach, you must decide to resist the urge to play only your "best" players in the quest of winning a pee-wee league championship. As a teacher, you must decide to hold athletes accountable to the same academic standards and expectations as nonathletes. As a college coach, you must decide that your and your institution's integrity are too important to sacrifice by cheating to recruit a pimply-faced high school football star.

To start, you must decide to ask questions. You must decide to challenge the heretofore unquestioned notions about sport's educational impact. And, the fundamental question is this: Is our investment in sport as a vehicle to produce positive educational outcomes generating the desired results?

About the Editor and Contributors

Dr. Darlene Bailey is Associate Athletic Director at Southwest Missouri State University. Previously, she was Senior Associate Athletic Director at Wichita State University, where her responsibilities included administration of various sports programs, oversight of the internal operation of the department, and the annual operating budget. She also served as NCAA compliance officer and was responsible for executing the institution's agreement with the U.S. Office of Civil Rights related to Title IX compliance. Her experience in athletics includes serving as a sports information director, athletic academic advisor, director of athletics, and interim vice president for student affairs. Bailey is a graduate of William Jewell College and holds an M.S. in Sports Administration and a Ph.D. in Higher Education, both from Ohio University.

Dr. Jennifer M. Beller, is a Research and Measurement Specialist, for the College of Education at the University of Idaho and is affiliate faculty member at the University of Idaho's Center for Ethics. She is the principal author of the *Hahm–Beller Values Choice Inventory in the Sport Milieu,* the definitive moral-reasoning instrument in use today for sports populations. Author of three texts and numerous articles, she has published, presented, and consulted in moral and character education and moral development in various competitive populations from business schools, law schools, the military, and schools of education. She earned her Ph.D. in Sports Ethics from the University of Idaho.

Bob Bigelow is a former four-year NBA player and first-round draft pick. He is a graduate of the University of Pennsylvania, where he was an All-American. Bigelow has made presentations to groups in over 250 communities throughout the United States on how to keep youth sports in perspective. He also coaches youth basketball, baseball and soccer.

Darren Bilberry attended the University of Kentucky on a football scholarship, where he earned Academic All-Southeastern Conference honors in 1989. He has worked as an academic advisor for student-athletes at Southern Illinois and Auburn Universities and served as the academic counselor for the football team at Kentucky. He currently is an academic advisor in the central advising and transfer center at Kentucky.

Dr. Michael Clark is a faculty member at Michigan State University's Institute for the Study of Youth Sports. Clark served in a number of capacities during more than 20 years of involvement with public schools in the Lansing area. In addition to teaching math and science, he served as an athletic administrator and coached several levels of boys' basketball as well as junior varsity softball. Clark conducts wide-ranging research on youth sports for the Institute and is responsible for outreach programs including coaches' clinics and education programs. He is also the primary author of the National Association for Sport and Physical Education's *National Standards for Athletic Coaches*. He also serves on NASPE's National Council for the Accreditation of Coaches Education Steering Committee. He continues his involvement in sports as a high school basketball referee and track starter.

Dr. Todd Crosset is an Assistant Professor of Sport Management at the University of Massachusetts, Amherst. His primary focus is the social world of athletes and social problems in sport. His book, *Outsiders in the Clubhouse: The World of Professional Women's Golf*, explores the life of LPGA golfers. He is a recognized authority on the problem of sexual assault in athletics. Prior to coming to UMass in 1993, Crosset served as head coach for the men's and women's swimming and diving teams at Northeastern University and as Assistant Athletic Director at Dartmouth College. He was an All-American swimmer at the University of Texas, Austin, and a member of their 1981 National Championship Team. He earned his M.A. in 1985 and his Ph.D. in 1992, both from Brandeis University.

Bill Curry has done it all in football. A three-year letterman at Georgia Tech, Curry was also an integral part of the Vince Lombardi Green Bay Packer teams that won the 1965 NFL Championship and the first Super Bowl in 1966. Curry played in Super Bowls III and VI as a member of the Baltimore Colts, and was named to the All-Pro Team in 1971 and 1972. After 10 years in the NFL, he began his coaching career at Georgia Tech. Following a 3-year stint as Offensive Line Coach with the Green Bay Packers, he returned to Georgia Tech in 1980 as Head Coach, where he was named ACC Coach of the Year in 1985 after guiding Tech to a 9–2–1 record. From Tech, he moved to the University of Alabama, where in 1989 his Crimson Tide team posted a 10–1 regular season record, shared the

SEC title, and earned him SEC Coach of the Year honors. Curry was then named Head Coach at the University of Kentucky, where his 1993 team posted a 6–5 record and earned a spot in the Peach Bowl, Kentucky's first bowl appearance in 9 years. Kentucky also led the SEC numerous times in academic honor role selections during his 7 years as Head Coach. Curry is currently a football analyst for ESPN.

Derrick Gragg is Assistant Athletic Director for Compliance at the University of Michigan. He came to Michigan from the University of Missouri, where he was Director of Compliance & Operations for the Tiger program. A former wide receiver at Vanderbilt University, Gragg served as Director of Student Life for Athletics at his alma mater before taking over compliance duties at Missouri. A Southeastern Conference all-academic choice, Gragg earned his B. S. from Vanderbilt in 1992. He attended the University of Tennessee Law School during 1992–93 before returning to Vanderbilt to begin his career in intercollegiate athletic administration.

Dr. Andrew Kreutzer is Coordinator of Ohio University's Sports Administration and Facility Management Program. Prior to assuming his role at Ohio in 1995, he served for 11 years at St. Thomas University in Miami, Florida. At St. Thomas, Kreutzer was, in succession, Director of Athletics, Chair of Sports Administration, and Director of the Division of Business, Economics, Sports Administration, and Tourism/Hospitality Management. He received his B.A. in Management from Eckerd College, and his M.A. in Sports Administration and Ph.D in Higher Education, both from Ohio University.

Robert (Bob) McCabe attended Harvard College, where he majored in government and played varsity basketball. Upon graduating in 1983, Bob played professional basketball in Europe. He joined the staff at Northeastern University's Center for Study of Sport in Society in 1990, as an original member of the Center's PROJECT TEAMWORK, an initiative to combat violence, racism, sexism, and anti-Semitism. Subsequent to his work with PROJECT TEAMWORK, he conducted a year-long study of intercollegiate athletics, the College Student-Athlete Program, funded by the U.S. Department of Education. Working with college presidents, athletic directors, coaches, and student-athletes, McCabe analyzed current approaches to academic oversight, athletic administration, community outreach, and student-athlete development in college athletic programs at seven NCAA Division I programs. McCabe also served as Director of the Center's Americore Athletes in Service to America, where he was responsible for the design, funding, and administration of the program at several colleges and universities across the country. The program features over 300 current and former collegiate student-athletes who provide workshops, tutoring, and mentoring at schools and community centers to reduce violence and enhance academic success.

After their football program received the "Death Penalty" for widespread NCAA violations in 1988, Southern Methodist University turned to **Dr. Cynthia M. Patterson** to develop and manage a comprehensive compliance and academic support program for the athletic department. An assistant athletic director at Northwestern University from 1984–1988, Patterson was charged with spearheading SMU's efforts to restore integrity to its athletic program. From 1992–1997, she held the position of Dean of Academic Advising and Co-Curricular Life at Sweet Briar College. Currently, she is Vice President for Academic Affairs and Dean of the College at Anna Maria College in Paxton, MA. Patterson earned her B.A. in History from Rollins College and Ph.D. in History from Northwestern.

Dr. Sharon Stoll is Professor of Physical Education and Director of the Center for Ethics, at the University of Idaho. A former public school teacher, coach, and athlete, she holds a Ph.D. in Sport Philosophy from Kent State University and is the creator and director of the only program in America that is dedicated to moral education with competitive populations. She is a winner of the prestigious University Award for Teaching at Idaho and has authored eight books, including *Who Says It's Cheating* and *Sports Ethics: Applications for Fair Play.*

Dr. John R. Gerdy, the editor, is a 1979 graduate of Davidson College, where he achieved All-American honors in basketball and had his jersey number retired. He played one season of professional basketball in the Continental Basketball Association. After earning a Masters in Sports Administration and a Ph.D. in Higher Education from Ohio University, he served as a Legislative Assistant at the NCAA from 1986–1989. Gerdy then moved to the Southeastern Conference, where he held the position of Associate Commissioner until 1995. He currently teaches as a visiting professor in Sports Administration at Ohio University. He previously authored *The Successful College Athletic Program: The New Standard*, published in 1997 as part of the American Council on Education/Oryx Press Series on Higher Education. He lives on a farm in Lancaster, Pennsylvania, with his wife and two children. His e-mail address is johngerdy@AOL.com.

Index